Cambridge Elements ≡

Elements in Modern Wars

WARRIOR WOMEN

The Cultural Politics of Armed Women, c.1850–1945

Alison S. Fell
University of Liverpool

CAMBRIDGE
UNIVERSITY PRESS

Shaftesbury Road, Cambridge CB2 8EA, United Kingdom

One Liberty Plaza, 20th Floor, New York, NY 10006, USA

477 Williamstown Road, Port Melbourne, VIC 3207, Australia

314–321, 3rd Floor, Plot 3, Splendor Forum, Jasola District Centre, New Delhi – 110025, India

103 Penang Road, #05–06/07, Visioncrest Commercial, Singapore 238467

Cambridge University Press is part of Cambridge University Press & Assessment, a department of the University of Cambridge.

We share the University's mission to contribute to society through the pursuit of education, learning and research at the highest international levels of excellence.

www.cambridge.org
Information on this title: www.cambridge.org/9781009069045

DOI: 10.1017/9781009070089

First published 2023

A catalogue record for this publication is available from the British Library.

ISBN 978-1-009-06904-5 Paperback
ISSN 2633-8378 (online)
ISSN 2633-836X (print)

Warrior Women

The Cultural Politics of Armed Women, c.1850–1945

Elements in Modern Wars

DOI: 10.1017/9781009070089
First published online: May 2023

Alison S. Fell
University of Liverpool

Author for correspondence: Alison S. Fell, asfell@liverpool.ac.uk

Abstract: This Element examines women warriors as vehicles of mobilisation. It argues that women warrior figures from the mid-nineteenth century until the end of the Second World War are best understood as examples of 'palimpsestic memory', as the way they were represented reflected new contexts while retaining traces of legendary models such as Joan of Arc, and of 'travelling memory', as their stories crossed geographical borders and were re-told and re-imagined. It considers the instrumentalisation of women warriors by both state actors to mobilise populations in the world wars and non-state actors in resistance, anti-colonial, and feminist movements. Fell's analysis of a broad range of global conflicts helps us to understand who these actors were, what motivated them, and what meanings armed women embodied for them, enabling a fresh understanding of the woman warrior as an archetype in modern warfare.

Keywords: woman warrior, war, gender, mobilisation, Joan of Arc

ISBNs: 9781009069045 (PB), 9781009070089 (OC)
ISSNs: 2633-8378 (online), 2633-836X (print)

Contents

1 The Cultural Politics of Armed Women

In 2017, coinciding with the centenary of the entry of the United States into the First World War, *Wonder Woman* was released to widespread critical acclaim and considerable commercial success.[1] The latest filmic re-imagining of American psychologist William Moulton Marston's 1941 cartoon superhero casts Israeli actor Gal Gadot as the saviour of the Allies in the final months of the war. *Wonder Woman* draws together elements from three familiar cultural scripts. First, it is a superhero origin story. To some extent, the film's female lead differentiates it from other post-9/11 superhero films that have been interpreted as cultural responses to perceived threats to American masculinity and national identity brought about by the 'war on terror' and shifting world and gender order.[2] Yet, mirroring many recent origin stories from the Marvel and DC franchises, the hero's backstory also revolves around the themes of loss, trauma, and destiny.[3] Second, Wonder Woman, or Princess Diana of Themyscira as she is named by her mother Hippolyta, is an archetypal woman warrior. Like Marston's 1941 original, which had been inspired by Ancient Greek and Roman mosaics and vases, she is part-Amazon, part-Goddess.[4] Furthermore, a key scene in which Wonder Woman defiantly leads Allied soldiers across No Man's Land (Figure 1) equally recalls two iconic nineteenth-century French Romantic versions of the woman warrior archetype, Eugène Delacroix's 1830 painting 'Liberty Leading the People', and François Rude's 1833 'Departure of the Volunteers of 1792' sculpture on the Arc de Triomphe, that both glorify the concept of a revolutionary citizenry mobilised by a symbolic female figure.[5] Third, *Wonder Woman* recalls dominant cultural visions of the Western Front as the site of an apocalyptic 'war to end all wars', in which innocent young male combatants and civilian women and children are the victims of a modern, industrialised war machine unleashed by incompetent and uncaring civilian and military leaders. However, unlike the majority of recent

---

[1] *Wonder Woman*, dir. P. Jenkins (2018). The film was awarded the 2018 Critics Choice Award for Best Action Movie, and has a score of 7.4/10 on www.imdb.com. To date, its cumulative gross worldwide box office takings are over $822 million.

[2] O. R. Horton, 'Origin Stories: Rebooting Masculinity in Superhero Films After 9/11', *Human: Journal of Literature & Culture*, 6 (2016), 72–85.

[3] A. J. Regalado, *Bending Steel: Modernity and the American Superhero* (Jackson, MS: University Press of Mississippi, 2015).

[4] Marston was also inspired by his support of women's rights and polyamorous relationship with his wife, psychologist Elizabeth Holloway who collaborated with him on experiments, writings, and in the creation of Wonder Woman, and Olive Byrne. J. Lepore, *The Secret History of Wonder Woman* (New York: Vintage, 2015); R. Schubart, 'Bulk, Breast and Beauty: Negotiating the Superhero Body in Gal Gadot's Wonder Woman', *Continuum*, 33:2 (2019), 160–72.

[5] It is significant in this context that the film's opening scenes take place in the Louvre museum. G. R. Denson, 'The Wonder Woman "No Man's Land" Scene Is Rooted in History, Myth and Art', *HuffPost*, 5 August 2017.

Figure 1 'Diana crossing No Man's Land', *Wonder Woman*, dir. P. Jenkins, 2017
Credit: Pictorial Press Ltd / Alamy Stock Photo

First World War films that foreground the victimhood of participants on both sides, the film also draws explicitly on tropes of Allied anti-German propaganda in its depiction of a demonic Ludendorff and his aide, the bitter facially disfigured chemist Dr Maru.[6] As a cruel, anti-maternal and scarred woman, Dr Maru functions in the film as the negative other of the brave, compassionate, and unblemished warrior-heroine.

Women warriors have always had a mixed reception. They have been praised by some as heroic models for both men and women to emulate, and attacked by others as aberrations. Similarly, *Wonder Woman* divided critics, particularly in terms of its feminist credentials. While Hilary Clinton stated that it was 'inspirational ... a movie about a strong powerful woman in a fight to save the world from international disaster', other critics argued that Wonder Woman had been reduced to a 'weaponised Smurfette', or saw her as a 'thin, white, cisgender able bodied Zionist', referring to Gadot's controversial background in and

---

[6] Her character is an amalgam of cultural representations of evil German chemists flouting the 1899 and 1907 Hague Conventions on the one hand, and of the treacherous and cruel German *femme fatale*-spy on the other, particularly the shadowy 'Fräulein Doktor', as depicted in the films *Mademoiselle Docteur*, dir. G. W. Pabst, 1937 and *Fräulein Doktor*, dir. A. Lattuada, 1969. The 'Fräulein Doktor' myth is often linked to Elsbeth Schragmüller, who trained spies, including Mata Hari. M. Walle, 'Fräulein Doktor Elsbeth Schragmüller', *Guerres mondiales et conflits contemporains*, 232 (2008), 47–58; T. Proctor, *Female Intelligence: Women and Espionage in the First World War* (New York: New York University Press, 2006).

ongoing support for the Israeli Defence Force.[7] Catherine Baker notes that by placing 'feminine' Amazonian values, which prioritise the preservation of life and harmony between nations and races, in opposition to the 'masculine' values of the God of War, Aries, whose lust for destruction is satisfied in the industrialised slaughter on the Western Front, the film was seen by some as a welcome change to the standard superhero narrative: 'Many women have described . . . the empowering pleasure of identifying with . . . Diana's shield-first bullet-deflecting charge through no man's land, or her more "desirable" and virtuous performance of war and diplomacy.'[8] Yet Wonder Woman is a problematic feminist heroine because of the film's uncritical adoption of other reductive stereotypes of female identity such as Dr Maru. In fact, as Susan Grayzel and Tammy Proctor comment, in *Wonder Woman* 'we mostly see women as victims' who 'stand in for the "innocent" lives that the new weapons of war destroy'.[9] The film's protagonist contains elements of different models of heroism derived from three cultural scripts that are the film's primary influences. Ultimately, like many cultural representations of modern warfare, it reproduces multiple – and, for feminist critics, contradictory – stereotypes of women and their relationship to war.

The reason I have begun this Element with *Wonder Woman* is because it illustrates how cultural representations of women warriors engaged in modern warfare are best understood as palimpsests. From the mid-nineteenth century to 1945, the period I focus on in this Element, female combatants included those who were recruited as women and those who 'passed' as men.[10] While the rarity of female combatants in this period made the women who were known to have borne arms highly visible, the ways in which they were depicted and written about often drew on myths and well-worn narratives, and did so in contradictory ways. In other words, representations of modern women warriors were certainly

---

[7] H. Clinton, email, 22 August 2017, https://still4hill.com/2017/08/22/email-from-hillary-clinton-4/; K. D. Killian, 'How Wonder Woman is and isn't a Feminist Superheroine Movie', *Psychology Today*, 19 June 2018, www.psychologytoday.com/gb/blog/intersections/201706/how-wonder-woman-is-and-isnt-feminist-superheroine-movie. Gad was a fitness instructor in the IDF and has voiced her ongoing support on social media, which led to the film being banned in Lebanon.

[8] C. Baker, 'A Different Kind of Power: Identification, Stardom and Embodiments of the Military in Wonder Woman', *Critical Studies on Security* 6:3 (2018), 359–65 (p. 361). https://doi.org/10.1080/21624887.2018.1432522.

[9] S. R. Grayzel and T. M. Proctor, 'Wonder Woman and the Realities of World War 1', https://blog.oup.com/2017/07/wonder-woman-and-world-war-i/.

[10] There have been several popular histories of women warriors covering broad timespans. These studies tend to offer narratives of individuals and usually present them as feminist heroines who defied patriarchal power structures and heterosexual/gender norms. See for example R. Cross and R. Miles, *Warrior Women: 3000 Years of Courage and Heroism* (London: Quercus, 2011); P. D. Toler, *Women Warriors: An Unexpected History* (Boston, MA: Beacon Press, 2019). Recent academic studies include J. Wheelwright, *Sisters in Arms: Female Warriors from Antiquity to the New Millennium* (London: Osprey, 2020) and B. Cothran, J. Judge and A. Shubert (eds.), *Women Warriors and National Heroes* (London: Bloomsbury, 2020).

grounded in their contemporary contexts, but they retained traces of the past. This was as true of female combatants' own memoirs as it was of romanticised interpretations of their life stories and military actions in popular culture. It was only in the decades following the end of the Second World War, when women began to be more commonly integrated into the military across the globe, that the associations between female combatants and existing cultural models of women warriors, such as the Amazons and Joan of Arc, were weakened.

The aim of this Element is to explore the ways in which the archetype of the woman warrior was adopted and adapted for political purposes in a broad range of global conflicts. It asks how and why representations of armed women were produced and circulated, how they were received, and what happened when they crossed borders. In doing so, it will focus on the key function of evocations of armed women in wartime: mobilisation.[11] Women warriors were used as inspirational figures in very different wars and conflicts across the globe, whether to encourage participation amongst the belligerent populations in the 'total wars' of the twentieth century, or to muster and justify resistance to foreign or imperial powers in periods of occupation or colonisation. Telling women warriors' stories thereby engaged a broad range of state and non-state actors, ranging from political and military leaders, religious authorities, activists, combatants and veterans, publishers and journalists to the readers and consumers of the numerous stories and images. Understanding who these actors were, what motivated them, and what meanings armed women embodied for them is crucial for an analysis of the cultural politics of the woman warrior.

In reality, female combatants were far outnumbered by women who performed support roles. The level of armed female participation was higher in civil, guerrilla, or other forms of unconventional warfare in which the distinctions between civilians and combatants were eroded.[12] But even in these conflicts the majority of women carried out logistical or healthcare functions. In military terms, this kind of work was the more significant; yet the *cultural* work performed by women warriors as galvanisers in wartime is undeniable. This period was a particularly prolific moment in the canonisation of new

---

[11] I follow John Horne's definition of mobilisation for the purposes of this study: 'the engagement of different belligerent[s] ... in their war efforts both imaginatively, through collective representations, and the beliefs and value systems giving rise to these, and organisationally, through the state and civil society'. J. Horne, 'Introduction', in J. Horne (ed.), *State, Society and Mobilisation in Europe in the First World War* (Cambridge: Cambridge University Press, 1997), pp. 1–18 (p. 1).

[12] For overviews of women's diverse roles in war, see K. Hagemann, S. Dudink and S. O. Rose (eds.), *Oxford Handbook of Gender, War and the Western World* (Oxford: Oxford University Press, 2021); B. C. Hacker and M. Vining (eds.), *A Companion to Women's Military History* (Leiden: Brill, 2012); R. Woodward and C. Duncanson (eds.), *The Palgrave International Handbook of Gender and the Military* (Basingstoke: Palgrave, 2017).

women warriors, including those I will consider in this Element: the 'Dahomey Amazons', Emilia Plater, Lalla Fatma N'Soumer, the Rani of Jhansi, Mekatilili wa Meza, Jeanne Merkus, Nene Hatun, Nana Yaa Asantewaa, Tringë Smajli, Constance Markievicz, Maria Bochkareva, Milunka Savić, Emilienne Moreau, Mexican *soldaderas*, Aleksandra Zagorska, Yoshiko Kawashima, *milicianas* in the Spanish Civil War, Lyudmina Pavlichenko, and Lela Karayanni.[13] The combination of the rise of nation-states and accompanying need for hero myths, the changing nature of warfare, revolutionary transformations in journalism and publishing and rising literacy rates, especially in Europe and North America, saw the proliferation and circulation of women warrior stories at a global scale. Provoking diverse reactions ranging between admiration, fascination, and alarm, these new warrior women exploded across different media. The rise of international news agencies in the second half of the nineteenth century was particularly significant as it enabled the stories of modern women warriors to cross borders.[14] This Element will reveal the power dynamics and complex entanglements – such as between state and non-state actors during wartime, and between the Western and non-Western worlds – that were at play in the production of these mobilising images and stories of women warriors.

1.1 Women's Military Roles

The reasons for women warriors' fame and visibility relate to the broader gender history of modern warfare. In the nineteenth century, the working-class women who had accompanied Western armies to cook, clean, sew, launder, and care for them gradually disappeared as armies professionalised. Support and auxiliary functions were taken over by men who were given a legitimacy and considered to be 'soldiers' in a way that had never been the case for women.[15] In the nineteenth century, most armies forbade the enlistment of women.[16] However, during the

---

[13] For biographical dictionaries of individual women warriors, see L. Grant de Pauw, *Battle Cries and Lullabies: Women in War from Prehistory to the Present* (Norman, OK: University of Oklahoma Press, 1998); R. Pennington (ed.), *From Amazons to Fighter Pilots*, 2 vols. (Westport, CT: Greenwood, 2003); J. A. Salmonson, *The Encyclopedia of Amazons: Women Warriors from Antiquity to the Modern Era* (St Paul, MN: Paragon House, 1991).

[14] Agence France-Presse developed from Agence Havas, founded in 1835. Associated Press was founded in 1846, Reuters in 1851, and Agenzia Stefani in 1855. War stories were particularly sought after and circulated by news agencies: in the United States, for example, the top international stories of the 1870s included the Franco-Prussian and Russo-Turkish Wars. M. B. Palmer, *International News Agencies: A History* (Basingstoke: Palgrave Macmillan, 2019), p. 48.

[15] G. J. Degroot, 'Arms and the Woman', in G. J. Degroot and C. Peniston-Bird (eds.), *A Soldier and a Woman: Sexual Integration in the Military* (London: Longman, 2000), pp. 3–17 (p. 8).

[16] J. Wheelwright, *Sisters in Arms*; T. Cardoza and K. Hagemann, 'History and Memory of Army Women and Female Soldiers, 1770s-1870s', in K. Hagemann, S. Dudink and S. O. Rose (eds.), *Oxford Handbook of Gender, War and the Western World* (Oxford: Oxford University Press), pp. 176–200.

American Civil War, for example, approximately 1,000 women enlisted in both the Confederate and Union armies. Although some newspapers admiringly described them as 'Amazons', they were frequently criticised. As Richard Hall summarises: 'gender conventions and prejudices of the mid-nineteenth century on the home front dictated that by virtue of their bold . . . behaviour, these women must be abnormal in some socially significant way'.[17] Feminist theorists of warfare have argued that this nineteenth-century gendering of roles and military zones has remained at the heart of the military and militarism throughout the twentieth century. Cynthia Enloe, one of the most influential thinkers in this field, argues that in modern warfare:

> The military plays a special role in the ideological structure of patriarchy because the notion of 'combat' plays such a central role in the construction of concepts of 'manhood' and justifications of the superiority of maleness in the social order. . . . Women – because they are *women*, not because they are nurses or wives or clerical workers – cannot qualify for entrance into the inner sanctum, combat.[18]

This model did not apply consistently in all contexts or all forms of warfare. As Karen Hagemann and Stefan Dudink point out, despite the emergence in nineteenth-century Europe of the association of the rights and duties of citizenship with male military service, 'citizenship was not masculinised to the same extent and in the same way everywhere – and the same thing holds true for the militarisation of masculinity'.[19] While European armies became almost exclusively male, there were styles of warfare elsewhere in the world that continued to include women. Some women were granted a form of warrior status in the Plains societies of North America. In parts of Africa, women had combat roles, including the most well-known and widely circulated example of the women who fought in the Franco-Dahomean Wars of 1890–4.[20] More common was the organisation of women into 'support cohorts' throughout eastern Africa, which

---

[17] R. Hall, *Women on the Civil War Battlefront* (Lawrence, KS: University Press of Kansas, 2006), p. 121.

[18] C. Enloe, *Does Khaki Become You? The Militarization of Women's Lives* (London: Pluto Press, 1983), pp. 12–15.

[19] K. Hagemann and S. Dudink, 'Masculinity and Politics in the Age of Democratic Revolutions 1750-1850', in K. Hagemann, S. Dudink and J. Tosh (eds.), *Masculinities in Politics and War: Gendering Politics and History* (Manchester: Manchester University Press, 2004), pp. 3–21 (p.19).

[20] The royal women of Dahomey had played significant political, religious, and military roles in the pre-colonial Kingdom of Dahomey. L. E. Larson, 'Wives and Warriors: The Royal Women of Dahomey as Representatives of the Kingdom', in J. Hobson (ed.), *The Routledge Companion to Black Women's Cultural Histories* (New York: Routledge, 2021), pp. 225–35; S. B. Alpern, *Amazons of Black Sparta: The Women Warriors of Dahomey* (New York: New York University Press, 1998).

resembled the tradition of laundresses, camp followers, and *cantinières* who had performed similar functions in the West.[21] Women also carried out support, logistics, and healthcare functions, as well as more limited combat duties, in revolutions, uprisings, and civil wars such as those that took place in Mexico (1910) and China (1911).

During the First World War, combat roles and war zones were still regarded and presented as the reserve of men, even as the realities of industrialised warfare provided a stark contrast to mobilising imagery of male combatant bravery, mastery, and *élan* on the battlefield.[22] These gendered boundaries were challenged during and after the war, both by the extent to which millions of civilians as well as combatants participated in (and were the victims of) 'total war', and by the mediatisation of militarised women. But across the combatant nations, the majority of women mobilised by governments or the armed services were deployed in non-combat roles: as nurses, or in transport, clerical, or domestic functions.[23] These women were subject to suspicion and criticism, especially those who were uniformed or given some form of military status such as the members of the women's auxiliary services in the British armed forces, which reveals the extent to which their work was seen as a potential threat to the status quo.[24] The civil wars, uprisings, and resistance movements that took place after the 1918 armistice, for example in Egypt, Ireland, Germany, Poland, and Russia, also included women, despite their marginalisation in some of the historiography.[25] Polish woman Aleksandra Zagorska, for example, formed the women's paramilitary organisation Ochotnicza Legia Kobiet (Voluntary Legion of Women) in November 1918, took part in the Polish-Soviet War (1919–21),

---

[21] B. C. Hacker, 'Reformers, Nurses, and Ladies in Uniform: The Changing Status of Military Women (c.1815–c.1914)', in B. Hacker and M. Vining (eds.), *A Companion to Women's Military History* (Leiden: Brill, 2012), pp. 137–88 (p. 154).

[22] J. Horne, 'Masculinity and Politics in the Age of Nation States and World Wars', in K. Hagemann, S. Dudink, and J. Tosh (eds.), *Masculinities in Politics and War*, pp. 22–40; K. Hagemann and S. O. Rose, 'War and Gender: The Age of the World Wars and its Aftermath', in K. Hagemann, S. Dudink and S. O. Rose (eds.), *Oxford Handbook of Gender, War and the Western World* (Oxford: Oxford University Press, 2021), pp. 369–409.

[23] S. R. Grayzel, *Women and the First World War* (London: Routledge, 2002); K. Jensen, 'Volunteers, Auxiliaries and Women's Mobilisation', in B. Hacker and M. Vining (eds.), *A Companion to Women's Military History* (Leiden: Brill, 2012), pp. 189–231.

[24] L. Noakes, *Women in the British Army: War and the Gentle Sex 1907–1948* (London: Routledge, 2006).

[25] J. Eichenberg, 'Soldiers to Civilians, Civilians to Soldiers: Poland and Ireland after the First World War', in R. Gerwarth and J. Horne (eds.), *War in Peace: Paramilitary Violence after the Great War* (Oxford: Oxford University Press, 2012), pp. 184–99; M. Stibbe and I. Sharp, '"In diesen Tagen kamen wir nicht von der Strasse." Frauen in der deutschen Revolution von 1918/ 19', *Ariadne* 73–74 (2018), 32–29; N. Ramdani, 'Women in the 1919 Egyptian Revolution: From Feminist Awakening to Nationalist Political Activism', *Journal of International Women's Studies* 14:2 (2013), 39–52; E. A. Wood, *The Baba and the Comrade: Gender and Politics in Revolutionary Russia* (Bloomington, IN: Indiana University Press, 1997).

and was promoted to the rank of Major.[26] From the 1920s onwards, Chinese women were enlisted to fight for Nationalist and Communist forces, creating as they did so 'a new social category of person – the woman soldier who wore a new-style military uniform and engaged in mechanised warfare'.[27] In Europe, women joined both fascist and anti-fascist paramilitary groups in the 1920s and 1930s, most notably the *milicianas* in the Spanish Civil War who engaged in armed combat.[28] Some of these women were able to argue for a form of post-war veteran status, including state pensions, but claims for a more permanent military status were mostly unsuccessful.[29]

The Second World War is often seen as a watershed moment which signalled a much broader acceptance of the necessity of integrating women into the military in industrialised mass warfare. From early in the war millions of women volunteered or were conscripted into war work in the belligerent nations and their empires. Thousands of women were drafted into combat roles in the Soviet Union, Eastern Europe, and Nazi Germany, where 160,000 women were working as Flak Gun auxiliaries by the end of the war.[30] Others actively participated in resistance movements in Axis-occupied Europe, or against the Japanese in China and Southeast Asia.[31] Yet Enloe's definition of the 'inner sanctum' of conflict as inherently bound up with concepts of masculinity still largely held true. In Britain, for example, this was illustrated in debates about women's entry into the Home Guard, which would have required them to be armed and was therefore seen as a step too far by the authorities.[32] Similarly, in underground and resistance movements, the women who bore arms continued

---

[26] S. Kuzma-Markowska, 'Soldiers, Members of Parliament, Social Activists: The Polish Women's Movement after World War 1', in I. Sharp and M. Stibbe (eds.), *Aftermaths of War: Womens' Movements and Female Activists 1918–1923* (Leiden: Brill, 2011), pp. 265–86.

[27] L. Edwards, *Women Warriors and Wartime Spies of China* (Cambridge: Cambridge University Press, 2016), p. 11.

[28] M. Nash, *Defying Male Civilization: Women in the Spanish Civil War* (Denver, CO: Arden Press, 1995).

[29] M. Vining, 'Women Join the Armed Forces: The Transformation of Women's Military Work in World War II and After', in B. Hacker and M. Vining (eds.), *A Companion to Women's Military History* (Leiden: Brill, 2012), pp. 233–89.

[30] K. Hagemann, 'History and Memory of Female Military Service in World Wars', in K. Hagemann, S. Dudink and S. O. Rose (eds.), *Oxford Handbook*, pp. 470–97 (p. 480).

[31] D. Campbell, 'Women in Combat: The World War II Experience in the United States, Great Britain, Germany and the Soviet Union', *Journal of Military History* 57:2 (1993), 301–23; B. Moore, *Resistance in Western Europe* (Oxford: Berg, 2000); N. Wingfield and M. Bucur (eds.), *Gender and War in Twentieth-Century Eastern Europe* (Bloomington, IN: Indiana University Press, 2006).

[32] P. Summerfield and C. Peniston-Bird, 'Women in the Firing Line: The Home Guard and the Defence of Gender Boundaries in Britain in the Second World War', *Women's History Review* 9:2 (2000), 231–55; J. A. Crang, *Sisters in Arms: Women in the British Armed Forces during the Second World War* (Cambridge: Cambridge University Press, 2021), p. 71.

to constitute a minority of resistant women as a whole, a fact that often led to an underestimation of their participation, as was the case in France.[33]

It was in this broader context that women warriors became the objects of both praise and approbation. Despite the widespread reluctance or refusal to accept female combatants within armies or armed resistance movements, women warriors were effective mobilisation vehicles. Examples of women carrying out combat roles demanded attention because of their difference from established gender norms. Their bearing of arms implied that the cause for which they were fighting was so important and so urgent that they were prepared to (temporarily) relinquish their 'natural' female roles and responsibilities to perpetrate violence, taking rather than giving life. In wartime, their defiance of broadly accepted understandings of men's and women's roles could be positively interpreted as proof of their valour and devotion to the cause. The stories and images of these modern women warriors were then frequently transposed onto familiar cultural models of armed female heroism such as the Amazons, Hua Mulan, Joan of Arc, and Agustina de Aragón, in order to fulfil their primary purpose of mobilisation.[34] This was not the case in peacetime, when they were most often viewed as disruptive or dangerous figures. The standard pattern during this period was therefore for female combatants to be heroised or martyrised during a war, when their representations served belligerents' purposes of mobilisation, nation-building, or resistance to occupation or oppression by a foreign power. Then, once the guns had fallen silent, they would be denigrated or forgotten. A common method of attacking and demonising women warriors both during and after conflicts was to question their sexual morality. Virginity was a key element of the persona of the woman warrior archetype; in turn, representing a woman warrior as sexually 'deviant', for example as lesbian or as a dangerous 'sexual predator', distanced them from affirmative models of armed female heroism.

---

[33] P. Schwartz, 'Behind the Lines: Women's Activism in Wartime France', in M. R. Higonnet, J. Jenson. S. Michel and M. Weitz (eds.), *Behind the Lines: Gender and the Two World Wars* (New Haven, CT: Yale University Press, 1987), pp. 141–53.

[34] See for example G. Cid, '"Amazons in the Pantheon?" Women Warriors, Nationalism and Hero Cults in Nineteenth and Twentieth-Century Chile and Peru', in B. Cothran, J. Judge and A. Shubert (eds.), *Women Warriors* (London: Bloomsbury, 2020), pp. 199–216; P. Davies, 'Women Warriors, Feminism and National Socialism: The Reception of J.J. Bachofen's view of Amazons among German and Austrian Right-Wing Women Writers', in S. Colvin and H. Watanabe-O'Kelly (eds.), *Women and Death 2: Warlike Women in the German Literary and Cultural Imagination Since 1500* (Rochester, NY: Camden House, 2000), pp. 45–60; K. Harris, 'Modern Mulans: Reimagining the Mulan Legend in Chinese Film 1920s–1960s', in E. Otto and V. Rocco (eds.), *The New Woman International: Representations in Photography and Film from the 1870s through the 1960s* (Ann Arbor, MI: University of Michigan Press, 2011), pp. 309–30; A. Shubert, 'Women Warriors and National Heroes: Agustina de Aragón and Her Indian Sisters', *Journal of World History* 23:2 (2012), 279–313.

During this period, industrialisation not only transformed the ways that wars were fought. It also had a significant impact on the dissemination of images of warfare. It enabled stories of modern women warriors to be discovered or re-discovered and circulated across the globe. These tellings and re-tellings consisted of illustrated postcards or photographic portraits (visual representations remained significant given the low levels of literacy in some parts of the world), articles or interviews in newspapers, published memoirs and novels, commemorative statues, poems, pieces of music, and other cultural performances. Different aspects of women warriors' personas were emphasised depending on the different political uses to which they were put. Despite the radical potential of female combatants to challenge the masculinisation of citizenship and militarisation of masculinity, women warriors were regularly evoked to promote conservative agendas in relation to gender roles and warfare. Examples of brave, patriotic female combatants were held up as a means of 'shaming' men into taking up their 'natural' roles as combatants. However, this fact does not mean that their potential to disrupt the gender and social order was completely lost. For example, women warriors were used throughout the late nineteenth and early twentieth centuries as figureheads for burgeoning women's movements, especially in Europe, the United States, Egypt, and China. In effect, women warriors proved to be malleable cultural figures that could be used to support opposing ideologies.

1.2 Joan of Arc and 'Travelling Memory'

To account for the global circulation of women warrior stories, a key concept within memory studies that this Element draws on is that of 'travelling memory'. Astrid Erll's work has explored the limitations of memory studies approaches that focus exclusively on the links between memory and the construction of national identities. She argues that Pierre Nora's concept of *lieux de mémoire*, for example, in 'bind[ing] memory, ethnicity, and the nation state together', fails to account for the fact that 'there are many fuzzy edges of national memory . . . [a] plethora of shared *lieux de mémoire* that have emerged through travel, trade, war and colonialism'.[35] The same might be said for some of the scholarship on the function of hero myths in relation to nation-building in modern Europe. Clearly, as Robert Gerwarth comments, the rise of hero myths in nineteenth- and twentieth-century Europe was 'intimately related to either the growing need of states to legitimate their existence or territorial shape, or the attempts of stateless (or occupied) nations to free themselves of foreign rule'.[36]

---

[35] A. Erll, 'Travelling Memory', *Parallax* 17:4 (2011), 4–18.

[36] R. Gerwarth, 'Introduction. Hero Cults and the Politics of the Past: Comparative European Perspectives', *European History Quarterly* 39:3 (2009), 381–87 (p. 384).

However, as Gerwarth also notes, there is an absence in the historiography 'of comparative studies that could help us identify international patterns of myth-making'.[37] Furthermore, hero myths often have significant cultural afterlives, crossing geographical borders and taking on lives of their own. It is in recognition of precisely this phenomenon that Erll proposes the concept of 'travelling memory', that she as defines as 'the incessant wandering of carriers, media, contents, forms and practices of memory, their continual "travel" and ongoing transformations through time and space, across social, linguistic and political borders'.[38] As the examples examined in this Element will show, this is a valuable theoretical tool for shedding light not only on why exceptional female combatants were the objects of fascination (or, in some cases, fetichisation) in the nineteenth and twentieth centuries, but more importantly also on how stories and images of some women warriors, such as the Rani of Jhansi and Emilia Plater, have travelled through time and space to serve different purposes for a range of state and non-state actors.

An important aspect of both palimpsestic and travelling memory that is immediately apparent in a global study of women warriors and their cultural afterlives in this period concerns the constant reference by European and North American journalists to Joan of Arc as the warriors' ultimate foremother. As Marina Warner shows in her landmark study, in the centuries since her death Joan of Arc has proven to be a tenacious and highly adaptable model of female heroism:

> [Joan of Arc] is literally a cypher. . . . In the transformations of her body, and in the different emphases of different times, we have a diviner's cup, which reflects on the surface of the water the image that the petitioner wants to see, its limits and extensions drawn, as in all magic operations of this kind, according to the known quantities shared between diviner and petitioner.[39]

In the nineteenth century, Joan of Arc remained the most popular point of reference in relation to contemporary women warriors. For example, Polish heroine Emilia Plater, who took part in the November Uprising (1830–1) that aimed to drive the Russian Empire out of partitioned Poland (present-day Lithuania), was presented as the 'Polish Joan of Arc' by a series of poets, playwrights, and political activists. In Adam Mickiewicz's famous 1832 poem 'The Death of the Colonel', Emilia was transformed from a Polish countess to a virginal heroine of the people, embodying national survival under foreign occupation: 'But this warrior though in a soldier's attire,/What a beautiful, maiden's face had he?/What breasts? – Ah, this was a maiden,/Lithuanian

---

[37] Ibid., p. 383.   [38] Erll, 'Travelling Memory'.
[39] M. Warner, *Joan of Arc: The Image of Female Heroism* (London: Penguin, 1983), p. 26.

born, a maiden-hero,/The leader of the uprising – Emilia Plater'.[40] The re-
tellings of the Plater story by Mickiewicz in the poem, and in his speech to the
Collège de France in 1842 to plead for the Polish cause in which he compared
Plater to the Maid of Orleans, were explicitly designed to appeal to international audiences already imbued in the cult of Joan of Arc.[41] Another
nineteenth-century female combatant who was given the epithet of Joan of
Arc was Dutch heiress Jeanne Merkus. In 1871, Merkus experienced the
violence of the Paris Commune when she cared for the sick and wounded in
Paris alongside high-profile French female revolutionaries such as Louise
Michel.[42] Two years later, Merkus donned a uniform adapted from local
dress and joined Serbian military commander Mićo Ljubibratić in the revolt
of the inhabitants of Herzegovina against the Ottoman Empire, motivated by
her religious faith, and by her own childhood idolisation of Joan of Arc.[43] In
March 1876, she returned to Belgrade after being imprisoned by Austrian
forces, and entered the city in triumph, riding a horse and wearing
a Montenegrin cap and man's cape. The Western press described her as the
'Joan of Arc of the Balkans' and 'the Amazon of Herzegovina'. During
a ceremony in Belgrade celebrating her heroism, a Serbian professor also
compared her to Joan of Arc in his speech, and Serbian poet and political
activist Georgije 'Đura' Jakšić wrote of her: 'Our Joan, not the one from
Orleans, yet her equal, as pure as an angel'.[44]

The tendency to compare modern women warriors to Joan of Arc continued
into the early decades of the twentieth century. In 1911, the world press
covered the story of Tringë Smajli Martini Juncaj, sometimes known as
Yanitza, who fought in the uprising against the Ottoman Empire that lasted
from March to August of that year in the Malësia region in Northern Albania

---

[40] English translation of 'The Death of a Colonel' quoted in E. Hauser, 'Traditions of Patriotism,
Question of Gender: The Case of Poland', in E. E. Berry (ed.), *Postcommunism and the Body
Politic* (New York: New York University Press, 1995), pp. 78–104 (p. 87). Hauser notes that the
poem has remained a staple of Polish school curricula.

[41] H. Filipowicz, 'The Daughters of Emilia Plater', in P. Chester and S. Forrester (eds.),
Engendering Slavic Literatures (Bloomington, IN: Indiana University Press, 1996), pp. 34–82.

[42] Louise Michel and other *communardes* were also regularly compared to Joan of Arc, or
described as Amazons, either to praise or demonise them: 'The female warrior and female orator
were heroic, dangerous, foolish and irrational, depending on their creators' political positions',
G. L. Gullickson, *Unruly Women of Paris: Images of the Commune* (Ithaca, NY: Cornell
University Press, 1996), p. 74.

[43] Wheelwright, *Sisters in Arms*, pp. 78–9.

[44] Anon, 'Lettre de Serbie', *Le Soir*, 25 August 1876; Wheelwright, *Sisters in Arms*, p. 194. From
1875 to 1877, more than 1,500 newspaper and magazine articles in twenty-one languages and
from twenty-seven countries reported on Merkus, and her actions were described in novels and
poems during her lifetime and afterwards. W. Van Den Bosch and R. Grémaux, 'Jeanne Merkus',
in *Digital Women's Lexicon of the Netherlands*, http://resources.huygens.knaw.nl/vrouwenlex
icon/lemmata/data/Merkus.

and eastern and central Montenegro. In May 1911, the *New York Times* printed an article with the headline 'Albanian Joan of Arc'.[45] In ethnographic mode, the article emphasises Smajli's femininity and military prowess: 'This new Joan of Arc is not yet 22 years of age . . . a tall, handsome and well-developed young woman. All the Albanian young women are brave, and are trained from their girlhood to the use of firearms.' The story was taken up in France by the populist newspaper *Le Petit Journal* that published a striking accompanying colour illustration (Figure 2). A few months later, a French illustrated children's newspaper presented Yanitza alongside female Mexican revolutionaries as members of a new breed of 'young warriors, worthy sisters of Joan of Arc' proving that 'feminine bravery is far from extinct and only needs the right occasion to reveal itself'.[46] The *Petit Journal* illustration featured the black and red colours of the Albanian flag, while the composition of the image also overtly referenced Delacroix's 'Liberty Leading the People' and Rude's 'Departure of the Volunteers of 1792', aligning the Albanian warrior with familiar French models of female revolutionary heroism. However, what was lost in these American and French cultural translations was the tradition of the Albanian *burrnesha*: individuals born biologically female who were permitted within the customary laws of the region (the 'Kanun of Leke Dukagjini') to live and be identified as men.[47] It seems clear that Smajli was a *burrneshe* who took on a prominent role in the 1911 uprising. *Burrnesha* were objects of fascination for Western travellers, who viewed Albania in the nineteenth and early twentieth centuries as wild and savage, with 'barbaric' customs, or as a population that the 'river of evolution' had left 'stranded', the view of British

---

[45] Anon, 'Albanian Joan of Arc: Handsome Heroine Takes Father's Place and Vanquishes Turks', *New York Times*, 21 May 1911. The story also appeared in British newspapers, extensively quoting Serbian statesman Čedomilj Mijatović, who stated: 'She is most truly a modern Maid of Orleans'. Anon, 'I Will Lead You', *Pall Mall Gazette*, 5 May 1911.

[46] Anon, 'Jeannes d'Arc', *La Jeunesse Illustrée*, 17 December 1911. The press coverage subsequently inspired 'Yanitza', a lyrical scene written by French librettist Georges Spitzmuller and set to music as a cantata by composers Paul Paray, who won the 1911 Premier Grand Prix de Rome, and Marcel Dupré. P. Paray, 'Yanitza, cantate avec orchestre', 1911, MS autogr., BNF, MS6457; M. Dupré, 'Yanitza, cantate pour 3 voix et orchestre', 1912, MS autgr., BNF, MS17634. Notably, Paul Paray also composed the Mass for the five hundredth anniversary of the death of Joan of Arc in 1931.

[47] *Burrnesha* did not solely take on a male identity to take up arms. Scholars have suggested that other possible motivations included avoiding an arranged marriage, the ability to inherit in the absence of a male heir, or the desire to escape the restrictive gendered expectations of women's roles. Their uses and preferences of names and gender pronouns varied, but some *burrnesha* may be understood as trans according to Rachel Mesche's broad definition: 'The broad category of trans can include anyone who feels misaligned with the gender attributed to them, regardless of how they identify and how they choose to express themselves'. R. Mesche, *Before Trans: Three Gender Stories from Nineteenth-Century France* (Redwood City, CA: Stanford University Press, 2020), p. 8; A. Young, *Women Who Become Men: Albanian Sworn Virgins* (Oxford: Berg, 2000).

Figure 2 'Yanitza, the Albanian Joan of Arc', *Le Petit Journal Supplément Illustré*, 28 May 1911

traveller Mary Edith Durham.[48] Within this orientalist optic, as Aleksandra Horváth demonstrates in an analysis of a 1907 account by German doctor

---

[48] A. K. Smith, *British Women of the Eastern Front: War, Writing and Experience in Serbia and Russia, 1914–20* (Manchester: Manchester University Press, 2016), p. 11; M. E. Durham, *High Albania* (London: Edward Arnold, 1909).

Ernst Schultz, Albanian *burrnesha* were re-interpreted for Western audiences as 'sworn virgins', thereby situating them firmly at one end of the virgin/ whore dichotomy through which women were judged.[49]

Rather than using orientalist stereotypes, however, the French *Petit Journal* journalist Ernest Laut associated 'Yanitza' with Western models of women warriors:

> Without speaking about the innumerable women whose taste for adventure led them to rush to take up arms, let us value those whose bellicose ardour was inspired by patriotism alone, those whose love for their country took them away from their families to transform them not only into warriors, but into heroines who inspire heroism, those who, in a word, are the true equals of Joan of Arc.[50]

Tellingly, Laut differentiates between 'adventuresses', who take up arms to satisfy individual desires, and 'the true equals of Joan of Arc', who sacrifice a feminised domestic role for patriotic reasons, and in doing so perform a crucial role as inspirers and mobilisers of others to their cause. This vision of Joan of Arc as a selfless, patriotic, and chaste young heroine whose example should be emulated was widespread on both sides of the political spectrum in early twentieth-century France, and neutralised the woman warrior's potential to symbolise a transgression of the gender and/or social order.[51]

Labelling a broad range of armed women as 'Joan of Arc', moreover, was not limited to European examples. Nana Yaa Asantewaa, an Asante Queen Mother who following the death of her brother played a key role in the 1900–1 Asante-British War (War of the Golden Stool), was regularly called 'Africa's Joan of Arc' in the British press.[52] In 1901, Michael White published a book about the

---

[49] Horváth also notes that Western travel accounts describing *burrnesha* contain echoes of late nineteenth- and early twentieth-century representations of '"Amazon" warrior women, [or] ethnic "wild women", like those of Dahomey and from the Kalmuks', who were displayed in dehumanising ethnographic exhibits. A. D. Horváth, 'Of Female Chastity and Male Arms: The Balkan "Man-Woman" in the Age of the World Picture', *Journal of the History of Sexuality*, 20:2 (2011), 358–81 (p. 370). See also A. D. Horváth, 'An Amazon Warrior, A Chaste Maiden or a Social Man? Early Ethnographic Accounts of the Balkan Man-Woman', *Aspasia* 3:1 (2009), 1–30.

[50] E. Laut, 'Les Emules de Jeanne d'Arc', *Le Petit Journal Supplément*, 28 May 1911.

[51] Warner, *Joan of Arc*, p. 249.

[52] Anon, 'A West African Joan of Arc', *Western Evening Herald*, 11 January 1896. This article claims the title was first used in a letter from Cecil Hamilton to his father. Hamilton served as an army officer on the Gold Coast from 1895 before becoming one of two District Commissioners in Asante, and wrote a narrative of the conflict in which Yaa Asantewaa plays a prominent role: C. Hamilton Armitage and A. Forbes Montanaro, *The Ashante Campaign of 1900* (London: Sands, 1901). A. Adu Boahen, *Yaa Asantewaa and the Asante-British War of 1900–1* (Accra: Sub-Saharan, 2003); N. Sackeyfio-Lenoch, 'Reframing Yaa Asantewaa through the Shifting

Rani of Jhansi, a leading figure in the Indian First War of Independence (Indian Mutiny) of 1857, entitled *Lachmi Bai: The Jeanne d'Arc of India*.[53] In 1933, the Australian *World's News* followed the example of other world newspapers when it ran a story about Yoshiko Kawashima entitled 'Japan's Joan of Arc'. Despite the headline, Kawashima's identity was complex: a Manchu princess brought up in Japan, Kawashima relinquished a female identity in 1925 and dressed and identified as a man. Kawashima spied for the Japanese Army before founding a counterinsurgency unit in 1932 to suppress anti-Japanese resistance in occupied Manchuria.[54] This tendency to use 'Joan of Arc' as a blueprint against which modern warriors were viewed and judged reveals a Western/non-Western power dynamic in relation to the images and stories of women warriors that were circulating around the globe. Comparing warriors to 'Joan of Arc' was a way of making a diverse range of individuals and political, cultural, and military contexts legible for the readerships of Western newspapers, and of controlling and limiting the meanings with which the warriors were charged. The nature of the individual conflicts, and of the diverse roles that the warriors played within them, is thereby smoothed over in favour of a Western model of feminised and patriotic Christian sacrifice.

The remaining sections of this Element consider in more detail the uses of women warrior figures in relation to their primary function as figures designed to inspire and influence the behaviour of others in wartime. Section 2 analyses the way images of armed women were used for mobilisation in the two world wars, focusing on visual culture in 1914–18 and the global circulation of depictions of Russian/Soviet women soldiers in both wars. Section 3 explores armed women as symbols of resistance in anti-colonial and feminist movements. First, it analyses the evolving depiction of the Rani of Jhansi, whose life and actions were depicted in contrasting ways after her death in, on the one hand, colonial and orientalist discourse and, on the other, as an icon of anti-colonial resistance. Second, it explores the varied uses of images of women-in-arms in global campaigns for female suffrage, including parades, pageants, books, and images, interrogating the complicated relationship between feminism, pacifism, and the uses of armed women as hero myths to popularise suffragist and/or feminist movements. Finally, the Element examines women

---

Paradigms of African Historiography', in J. Hobson (ed.), *The Routledge Companion to Black Women's Cultural Histories* (New York: Routledge, 2021), pp. 236–44.

[53] M. White, *Lachmi Bai: The Jeanne d'Arc of India* (New York: J.F. Taylor, 1901).

[54] Anon, 'Japan's Joan of Arc', *The World's News* (Sydney), 22 November 1933. Notably, and because of her history as a spy, she was also labelled the 'Mata Hari of the East'. Kawashima was imprisoned during the Chinese Civil War, and executed in 1948. Edwards, *Women Warriors*; P. Birnbaum, *Manchu Princess, Japanese Spy: The Story of Yoshiko Kawashima, the Cross-Dressing Spy who Commanded Her Own Army* (New York: Columbia University Press, 2017).

warriors in relation to demobilisation and post-war memory cultures. Section 4 considers the ways that female ex-combatants themselves attempted – successfully or unsuccessfully – to instrumentalise their wartime profiles for personal, economic, or political purposes. Some of the warriors who feature in this Element have been examined individually by scholars, but rarely from a transnational perspective. This Element responds to the recent observation made by Boyd Cothran, Joan Judge, and Adrian Shubert that 'it is necessary to widen the lens of analysis beyond the specific nation-states from within which the stories [of women warriors] have typically flourished'.[55] In order to widen the lens in this way, I draw on several excellent studies of individual women warriors, but add to their conclusions by including additional examples, and by placing individual case studies in robust conversation with one another.[56]

2 Women Warriors and Mobilisation in the World Wars

War propaganda was not a new phenomenon in the twentieth century, but it played a particularly important role during the industrialised mass warfare of the two world wars, in which empires and states had to mobilise the support of whole societies and their economies. The development of mass and multimedia provided the means for the widespread dissemination of propaganda, and helped it to become an essential tool in the waging of total war.[57] In both conflicts, and across all belligerent nations, military masculinity was omnipresent and was used as a means of motivating and reassuring both combatants and civilians. In terms of gender politics, war propaganda usually belied the realities of the blurring of boundaries between men's and women's roles, and between civilian and combatant, or home and front, promising instead 'either a return to the prewar gender order based on the male breadwinner-female homemaker family or a new order of society based on social and gender equality'.[58] However, in wartime visual culture civilian life was often militarised: visual cues and military language transformed the traditionally feminised domestic sphere into an extension of the war zone, and women's waged or unwaged labour into patriotic war work, a female equivalent of male military service.[59]

---

[55] Cothran, Judge and Shubert (eds.), 'Introduction', p. 3.

[56] In a book of this length it is necessary to be selective. Although I have endeavoured to include a broad range of case studies from across the globe, some female combatants, for example those involved in Latin American revolutionary movements, receive less attention than others.

[57] J. Fox and D. Welch, 'Justifying War: Propaganda, Politics and the Modern Age', in D. Welch (ed.), *Justifying War: Propaganda, Politics and the Modern Age* (Basingstoke: Palgrave Macmillan, 2012), pp. 1–21.

[58] Hagemann and Rose, 'War and Gender', p. 387.

[59] P. James, 'Images of Femininity in American World War I Posters', in P. James (ed.), *Picture This: World War 1 Posters and Visual Culture* (Lincoln, NE: University of Nebraska Press, 2009), pp. 273–311 (p. 292).

Furthermore, not all images of women in the world wars featured them in traditional or domestic roles. Female combatants were regularly used to aid mobilisation, but their characteristics and meanings varied considerably. In the thousands of posters, postcards, and illustrations that circulated within and between belligerent nations during the world wars, images of armed women performed diverse functions: as patriotic embodiments of nation, as playful, romanticised, or sexualised militarised women designed to amuse or to titillate, or as heroised soldiers temporarily abandoning their 'feminine' roles for the sake of their nations, and encouraging men and women to follow their lead.

2.1 Visual Culture and Mobilisation in the First World War

The visual culture of the First World War demonstrates how industrialised war simultaneously shored up and challenged pre-existing understandings of how and why wars were fought, and of what men's and women's roles were within them. As Pearl James observes, this is evident in both the style and the content of wartime imagery: 'In war posters, new national identities coalesce around nostalgic visions of the past. Women wear both traditional and non-traditional guises. . . . Posters proffer a complex blend of folk art, traditional "high" art, and slick advertising sense'.[60] This blend of the traditional and the modern can equally be seen in First World War posters and postcards featuring women warriors. There exist numerous examples of mythical or classical armed female figures embodying nations such as Britannia, Germania, Italia, and Marianne, or 'universal' values such as Justice, Liberty, and Victory.[61] However, the success of these idealised allegorical figures depended on the 'unlikelihood of women practising the concepts they represented': they remained in the symbolic order, detached from the real world.[62] Joan of Arc was also prominent in the First World War propaganda as an idealised embodiment of chaste and selfless patriotism, and played a key role in the mobilisation of both men and women. This was particularly the case in the United States, where she had enjoyed enormous popularity from the 1880s onwards, and inspired hundreds of works of art.[63] In 1915, Anna Vaughn Hyatt's statue of Joan of Arc was unveiled in New York, and was used as a gathering place to support American soldiers, and to celebrate the 1918 armistice. In 1916, Cecil B. de Mille released the film *Joan*

---

[60] P. James, 'Introduction: Reading World War I Posters', in P. James (ed.), *Picture This* (Lincoln, NE: University of Nebraska Press, 2009), pp. 1–36 (pp. 2–3).

[61] M. Rickards, *Posters of the First World War* (London: Evelyn, Adams and Mackay, 1968).

[62] M. Warner, *Monuments and Maidens: The Allegory of the Female Form* (London: Random House, 2010), p. 4.

[63] N. M. Heimann and L. Coyle, *Joan of Arc: Her Image in France and America* (Washington, DC: Corcoran Gallery of Art, 2006), pp. 68–71; C. Grimel, 'The American Maid', in D. Goy-Blanquet (ed.), *Joan of Arc: A Saint for All Seasons* (London: Ashgate, 2013), pp. 123–41.

the Woman, with a script by Jeannie MacPherson, which promoted American entry into the war. The film begins in 1916, and features the appearance of a ghostly Joan, 'the Girl Patriot', before a British officer in his trench, inspiring him to fight. As the inter-title explains to the spectators: 'Joan of Arc is not dead. She can never die – and in the war-torn land she loved so well her spirit fights today'.[64] In 1918, the Treasury Department exploited the success of Joan of Arc as a mobilising symbol of popular wartime patriotism in a poster designed by Haskell Coffin, which depicts a curvy Joan of Arc with sword held aloft and the accompanying message 'Joan of Arc Saved France. Women of America – Save Your Country. Buy War Savings Stamps' (Figure 3). The poster was aimed at a civilian audience, its romanticised imagery suggesting, as Claude Grimel remarks, that 'frugality in the household is tantamount to bravery on the battlefield'.[65] There is evidence that Coffin's poster inspired American women to participate in overseas war service. One cohort of war workers who

Figure 3 'Joan of Arc saved France', Poster, H. Coffin, 1918

---

[64] *Joan of Arc*, dir. C.B. De Mille, 1916.

[65] Grimel, 'The American Maid', p. 134. A similar poster was produced in Britain to promote war savings certificates. 'Joan of Arc Saved France', Poster, 1918, IWM, Art.IWM PST10297.

responded to Joan of Arc as a symbol of female patriotism were the 'Hello Girls', 223 bilingual female telephone switchboard operators who were trained and sent to the Western Front in 1918 to improve the performance of the US Army's telephone networks.[66] In the 1918 San Francisco War Bond Parade, the Hello Girls rode in a car bearing the slogan 'We are on our way to France to serve our country', and were flanked by a woman dressed as Joan of Arc riding a white horse, reminiscent of suffragist parades. Furthermore, in a surviving photograph of two members of the corps, sisters Raymonde and Louise Breton have a copy of Haskell's Joan of Arc poster prominently displayed on the wall of their barracks at Neufchâteau.[67]

Another very different image of armed women common in the First World War presented them as sentimentalised or sexualised uniformed combatants, who functioned as promised sexual rewards for recruits. American artist and illustrator Howard Chandler Christy produced some of the most frequently reproduced examples, such as the 1918 Naval Reserve Coastal Guard recruitment poster 'Gee!! I Wish I were a Man', in which a woman in navy uniform has a 'curve-accentuating pose, ... plunging neckline and ... sidelong, coquettish gaze' that issue a sexual invitation.[68] Similar evocations of female combatants existed in all the belligerent nations in popular postcards, such as the series by Italian illustrator Adolfo Busi picturing scantily-clad pin-up models wearing military uniforms, and firing hearts from rifles, canons and grenades, or the French 'Les Femmes soldat' series, featuring highly stylised, shapely high-heel-wearing female soldiers (Figure 4). Such images drew on the popularity of male impersonators who had regularly appeared on stage from the 1860s onwards in European and American theatres and music halls, often dressed as soldiers, such as British music hall performer Vesta Tilley, whose song 'The Bold Militiaman' (1897) promised her male listeners sexual favours in return for military duty.[69]

The reception of these kinds of images is hard to gauge. Scholars have effectively argued against a view of belligerent populations as 'blind pawns', helpless in the face of propaganda, that exaggerates its effectiveness and does not account for the different ways in which audiences would have identified (or not) with the messages being disseminated.[70] A more nuanced understanding of

---

[66] E. Cobbs, *The Hello Girls: America's First Women Soldiers* (Cambridge, MA: Harvard University Press, 2017).

[67] National Archives and Records Administration, College Park, Maryland, 111-SC-50699, reproduced in Cobbs, *The Hello Girls*.

[68] James, 'Images of Femininity', p. 290.

[69] E. Aston, 'Male Impersonators in the Music-Hall: The Case of Vesta Tilley', *New Theatre Quarterly* 4:15 (1988), 247–57.

[70] T. Paddock, 'Introduction', in T. Paddock (ed.), *World War 1 and Propaganda* (Leiden: Brill, 2014), pp. 1–17.

Figure 4 'Russie. Pour Dieu & Pour le Tzar' (Russia. For God & the Tzar),
French First World War postcard, A. Noyer

visual culture in the First World War that aimed to mobilise belligerent populations is provided by Annette Becker and Stéphane Audoin-Rouzeau: 'What is
called propaganda was not just a vertical process but also a horizontal one, even,
to some extent, a great upsurge from below, sustained by . . . illustrators . . .,
journalists, writers, film-makers, musicians and artists'.[71] This was certainly
true in relation to images of women dressed as soldiers. For example, the
popular figure of 'Fräulein Leutnant' had featured in pre-war Austrian and
German popular songs and operettas before being the subject of two wartime

---

[71] A. Becker and S. Audoin-Rouzeau, *1914–1918: Understanding the Great War* (London: Profile
Books, 2002), p. 109.

Figure 5 'Fräulein Leutnant', German First World War postcard. Caption:
'Wenn ich erst kommandiere/Zum sturm die infant'rie/Geht gern mit mir
durches Feuer/Die ganze kompagnie' (If I first command the infantry to attack,
the whole company will gladly advance under fire with me)

films directed by Carl Wilhelm, and a series of patriotic postcards (Figure 5).[72]
In German and Austrian 'Fräulein Leutnant' postcards, overt references to the
theatre, including phrases from popular pre-war songs and plays that appeared
as captions, set the tone for those who sent or received the cards, and positioned
the uniformed women as coquettish performers of a well-known theatrical type
who did not threaten the dominance of martial masculinity.[73] Rather, as Bettina
Brandt argues, the humorous staging emphasised both the support of the home

---

[72] *Fräulein Leutnant*, dir. C. Wilhelm, 1914; *Fräulein Feldgrau*, dir. C. Wilhelm, 1915.

[73] S. Giesbrecht, 'Deutsche Liedpostkarten als Propagandamedium im Ersten Weltkrieg', in
M. Matter and T. Widmaier (eds.), *Lied und Populare Kultur/Song and Popular Culture.
Jahrbuch des Deutschen Volksliedarchivs*, 50/51 (2006), 55–98.

front for mobilised combatants, and the distance of the stylised female figures from 'the male domain of serious fighting'.[74]

Yet the meanings of such images were always double-edged, as they had the potential to embody a sexual reward for combatants, and at the same time to threaten the status quo by referencing the wartime incursion of women into military roles. Thus, a 1916 British *Punch* cartoon was able to play on the cultural anxieties brought about by uniformed women for comic effect, mocking women soldiers by implying that as soon as the 'Amazon corps' had finished their drill exercises they reverted to stereotypically feminine behaviour that indicated their unsuitability for military service, such as putting on lipstick and adjusting their hairstyles.[75] Moreover, as David Boxwell argues, cross-dressing during the war, whether that was male impersonators in films and on stages behind the lines, or female impersonators in theatrical performances at the front, simultaneously neutralised and energised the possibility of same-sex desire, and thereby remained an inherently ambiguous performance of gender and sexuality.[76]

A final way in which militarised women appeared in First World War visual culture was as photographs or realist illustrations of heroised female combatants, designed to 'shame' men into enlisting, or to inspire women into non-combatant war work. For example, photographs of the uniformed members of the Women's Voluntary Reserve (WVR), a British paramilitary organisation, appeared in the Polish, French and American press.[77] The Warsaw daily newspaper *Bluszcz* described them as 'women-soldiers commanded by Colonel Lady Castlereagh', referring to the WVR's founder, Edith Vane-Tempest Stewart, the 7th Marchioness of Londonderry. The article made it clear, however, that their example was cited not in a bid to encourage Polish women to take up military or paramilitary roles, but to engage in gender-appropriate war work.[78] This was in line with the WVR's own

---

[74] B. Brandt, 'Germania in Armor: Female Representation of an Endangered German Nation', in S. Colvin and H. Watanabe-O'Kelly (eds.), *Women and Death 2: Warlike Women in the German Literary and Cultural Imagination Since 1500* (Rochester, NY: Camden House, 2000), pp. 86–126 (p. 104).

[75] 'Our Amazon corps "standing easy"', C. A. Shepperson, *Punch*, 26 April 1916. For a helpful discussion of the ways in which militarised women in the First World War had to negotiate the public's voyeuristic fascination with their activities alongside widespread hostility to their uniformed identities, see J. Pattinson, *Women of War: Gender, Modernity and the First Aid Nursing Yeomanry* (Manchester: Manchester University Press, 2020), chapter 2.

[76] D. A. Boxwell, 'The Follies of War: Cross-Dressing and Popular Theatre on the British Front', *Modernisms/Modernity* 9:1 (2002), 1–20.

[77] Anon, 'Les femmes à l'armée', *Excelsior*, 28 April 1915; Anon, 'English Women Aid in Getting Recruits', *New York Times*, 26 June 1915. A 1917 Pathé news-reel captured them marching through London: 'Women's Volunteer Reserve Marching', Pathé film, 1917, www .britishpathe.com/video/womens-voluntary-reserve-marching.

[78] R. Blobaum and D. Blobaum, 'A Different Kind of Home Front: War, Gender and Propaganda in Warsaw, 1914-1918', in T. Paddock (ed.), *World War 1 and Propaganda* (Leiden: Brill, 2014), pp. 249–72 (p. 261).

self-presentation, as they attempted to counter British press criticism of their uniforms and drill.[79] In a speech delivered in 1915, the Marchioness of Londonderry declared that the members of the Reserve 'were diametrically opposed' to 'ostentatious displays [of] women stamping up and down the country, bristling with firearms and making themselves ridiculous'.[80] Rather, she presented them as taking over the civilian duties of mobilised men. Other mediatised armed women included those involved in resistance networks in German-occupied France and Belgium, such as seventeen-year-old Emilienne Moreau in Loos-en-Gohelle, near Lens.[81] During the 1915 Battle of Loos, Moreau told the British about German gun placements, and allegedly killed at least two Germans with a British army revolver. Moreau's story had all the ingredients the press was looking for, and *Le Petit Parisien* quickly offered her 5,000 Francs for an exclusive. Her photograph and portrait in mourning clothes (her father and brother had died during the war) featured widely in the Allied press, and she was the subject of an Australian recruitment film in 1916, *The Joan of Arc of Loos*, directed by George Willoughby.[82] One Sydney newspaper reported that at the point in the film when, inspired by the vision of an Angel of War and waving the French flag, Moreau rallies the retreating Allies back into attack, 'the French section of the audience stood up and sang the Marseillaise'.[83] Other newspaper reports, however, were critical of the film's glorification of the battle, reflecting the wider debate over conscription in Australia. In France, Moreau was represented as much as a civilian as a combatant, symbolising stoicism in relation to the heavy losses of life and territory, the bravery, resistance and sacrifices made by patriotic civilians, and Allied cooperation under fire. Moreover, the contradictions apparent in the construction of a war heroine who combined innocent civilian war victim with patriotic woman warrior were not lost on the German press. *Des deutschen Volkes Kriegstagebuch* reproduced the French press photograph of Moreau with the caption 'The so-called "Heroine of Loos" who is being celebrated in the English and French press because she murdered five German soldiers in the Battle of Loos', strategically placed next to an article stressing the German nation's desire for peace.[84] Here, Moreau was

[79] The press attacked them for 'parading the streets in breeches' and 'masquerading as men'. Edith Londonderry, 'The Women's Legion, 1914', 1944, PRONI, D3099/14/1. Quoted in F. Walsh, *Irish Women and the Great War* (Cambridge: Cambridge University Press, 2020), p. 18.

[80] Ibid.

[81] A. S. Fell, *Women as Veterans in Britain and France after the First World War* (Cambridge: Cambridge University Press, 2018), pp. 71–9.

[82] A. Pike and R. Cooper, *Australian Film 1900–1977: A Guide to Feature Film Production* (Oxford: Oxford University Press, 1998), pp. 62–3.

[83] Anon, 'Joan of Arc of Loos', *Sydney Evening News*, 2 May 1916; 'The Joan of Arc of Loos: Original Release', 1916, 572222, National Film and Sound Archive of Australia.

[84] Anon, *Des deutschen Volkes Kriegstagebuch* (Leipzig: Philipp Reclam, 1915), p. 1009. Quoted in Fell, *Women as Veterans*, p. 75.

presented as an example of a *franc-tireur* breaking the rules of warfare rather than a model of patriotic female heroism for others to emulate.

2.2 Russian Women Soldiers

The use of images of armed women as a means of inspiring and/or 'shaming' non-mobilised men and women was particularly evident in both world wars in relation to the global circulation of images of Russian/Soviet women soldiers. In 1917, four women's battalions, two of which were known as Battalions of Death, and eleven communications detachments were established by the Provisional Government. A further ten all-female combat units were formed in units around the Russian Empire, but without official sanction, through the organisational efforts of local women's groups.[85] In total, between four and five thousand women served in the war, including one all-female naval unit.[86] The First Russian Women's Battalion of Death was led by Maria Bochkareva, a semi-literate peasant woman from Siberia who had been given special dispensation in 1914 to join the Russian army. Bochkareva was one of hundreds of Russian women who volunteered to become soldiers in the early years of the war. They were regularly compared by Russian journalists to the Amazons and Joan of Arc, both positively and negatively, echoing other press responses to high-profile European women soldiers, such as Milunka Savić and Flora Sandes in Serbia, or Dorothy Lawrence and Marie Marvingt, who both briefly fought for the British and French armies by 'passing' as men.[87] The establishment of the all-female units in 1917 should therefore not be understood as an indication of a widespread acceptance by the Russian public or Russian authorities of women in combat roles within the armed forces. Rather, their formation was in part an attempt by the Provincial Government after the February Revolution to address a national emergency, and in part the result of efforts by groups of women with shared goals and intentions, spearheaded by progressive women seeking greater participation of women in the public sphere. By mid-April, both military and civilian authorities were profoundly concerned about the fighting capacity of Russia's troops, and in May 1917 mass mutinies began to occur at the front.

---

[85] I am very grateful to the anonymous reviewer for their insightful comments on this section.

[86] M. K. Stockdale, "My Death for the Motherland Is Happiness": Women, Patriotism and Soldiering in Russia's Great War', *The American Historical Review* 109:1 (2004), 78–116; L.S. Stoff, *They Fought for the Motherland: Russia's Women Soldiers in World War 1 and the Revolution* (Lawrence, KS: University Press of Kansas, 2006).

[87] Lawrence, a journalist, published an account of her experience after the war: *Sapper Dorothy Lawrence: The Only English Woman Soldier, late Royal Engineers, 51st Division, 179th Tunnelling Company, BEF* (London: John Lane, 1919). There is photographic evidence that Marvingt served for a few weeks with the 42nd Battalion of the Chasseurs à Pied, as she claimed to have done in later interviews. See M. Cordier and R. Maggio, *Marie Marvingt: La Femme d'un Siècle* (Sarreguemines: Pierron, 1991).

Female soldiers were seen as one of the solutions to the problem by Alexander Kerensky, Minister of War. In the midst of a highly unstable political crisis, the women's battalions can be understood, as Laurie Stoff explains, as 'a bold social experiment undertaken largely for propaganda purposes … to serve as inspirational symbols to boost morale among the war-weary troops and simultaneously to shame men into resuming their "patriotic duty" as defenders of the nation'.[88]

Bochkareva fully embraced her role as the figurehead for the Provisional Government's attempt to mobilise Russian men and women in an increasingly unpopular war. Posters appeared with her photograph urging Russian women 'to join the general effort for victory over the enemy', and further images of her in uniform and wearing medals as proof of her bravery and service to the nation were published in newspapers and journals, for example in the journal *Russkoe slovo* produced in the United States by anti-tsarist Russian émigré Ivan Kuz'mich Okuntsov (Figure 6). Recruitment drives at theatres and other public venues starred Bochkareva declaring: 'To create real soldier-women and to go with them to the front … must serve to shame those male deserters, who, on the eve of final victory over the enemy, run away from their civic duty. … And so, comrades, I ask you to join my battalion'.[89] The appeal was successful and thousands of women came forward to offer their services, although not all were accepted. On 21 June 1917, Bochkareva and 300 members of the First Russian Women's Battalion of Death marched from their barracks to St Isaak's Cathedral in Petrograd, where their battalion was consecrated by Bishop Andrei of Ufa, and they were presented with a banner sent by Kerensky, featuring St George and a skull and crossbones.[90] The Marseillaise was played during this public spectacle, echoing Kerensky and the Provisional Government's beliefs that 'the noble symbols and images of the 1789 French Revolution would inspire Russian soldiers to the noble bellicosity of the soldiers of the French Revolution'.[91] Others referred specifically to the roles of women during the French Revolution in an effort to mobilise women, such as socialist war nurse Tatiana Aleksinskaia, whose pamphlet 'Women, War and Revolution' celebrated the contributions of French revolutionary female citizens to national defence.[92] To some extent, this was successful as a recruitment strategy, at least among young women. Ernest Poole, an American living in Russia, quoted a teenage girl linking her intention to enlist in the women's battalion with the French revolutionary precedent: 'How horrible it would be to

---

[88] Stoff, *They Fought for the Motherland*, p. 3.   [89] Ibid., p. 77.
[90] Stockdale, 'My Death for the Motherland', p. 78.
[91] D. Shlapentok, 'The Images of the French Revolution in the February and Bolshevik Revolutions', *Russian History* 16:1 (1989), 31–54 (p. 35).
[92] Stockdale, 'My Death for the Motherland', pp. 94–95.

Figure 6 'Head of the women's infantry battalion, Bochkareva', *Iskri* (Sparks),
Weekly Supplement of *Russkoe Slovo* (The Russian Word), Vol. 24, 1917

look back and say, "I was young at a time like the French Revolution, but all
I did was to ... stay in a nice, quiet place on a river!"'[93]

---

[93] E. Poole, *Russian Impressions* (New York: Macmillan, 1918), p. 148. Quoted in Shlapentok, 'The Images of the French Revolution', p. 38.

However, Bochkareva's women soldiers only briefly embodied the spirit of Rude's 'Departure of the Volunteers of 1792' leading reluctant Russian soldiers towards enemy trenches at the Battle of Novospassky Forest on 9–10 July 1917, in an attack that left two women dead, two missing, and thirty-six wounded.[94] The First Russian Women's Battalion of Death's military service, alongside its members' positive reputation as 'warriors' who could save the nation, were short-lived. In the following months, Russian women soldiers met with criticism, hostility, and failure. They were attacked by troops who blamed them for helping to prolong the fighting, and by the Bolsheviks for abandoning their femininity and being dupes of the bourgeoisie. In October 1917, a small number of women from the First Petrograd Women's Battalion took part in the defence of the Winter Palace, and were branded as counter-revolutionaries, although in reality women soldiers joined both sides in the Civil War.[95] Bochkareva joined the anti-Bolshevik cause and went to the United States, where she dictated her memoir, *Yashka*, before being tried and executed by the Bolsheviks in 1920.[96]

Images of Russian women soldiers also circulated globally, both as objects of fascination and as tools of mobilisation, and made Bochkareva an international media celebrity.[97] As had been the case with Albanian Tringë Smajli Martini Juncaj, some Western journalists linked the formation of the battalion with cultural stereotypes of the savagery or exoticism of Eastern European culture, seeing Russian peasant women as physically better suited to combat, or Russian women as revolutionary in nature.[98] The French newspaper *Le Miroir* published photographs that provided a striking contrast with the eroticised imagined Russian woman soldier in Figure 4, showing them in their uniforms and shaven heads during a physical training exercise in their barracks.[99] The caption reads: 'Here are the Russian women soldiers learning how to wrestle to develop their muscles', and the journalist noted the frequently repeated claim that the soldiers 'carried poison in case they were taken prisoner'. However, the Russian women warriors were not presented in the Western press as examples to follow, but as

---

[94] Stoff, *They Fought for the Motherland*, p. 106.

[95] Between 70 and 80,000 women are estimated to have served with the Red Army, the majority serving in support roles. High-profile female Red Army combatants included Rozaliia Samoilovna Zemliachka, a senior military commissar on the Southern Front and Northern Front who was nicknamed 'Bloody Rosa' by the British opposition. K. McElvanney, 'Women and the Russian Revolution', www.bl.uk/russian-revolution/articles/women-and-the-russian-revolution.

[96] M. Botchkareva and I. D. Levine, *Yashka: My Life as Peasant, Officer and Exile* (New York: Frederick A. Stokes, 1919).

[97] Wheelwright, *Sisters in Arms*, p. 61.   [98] Stoff, *They Fought for the Motherland*, p. 190.

[99] Anon, 'La vie des héroïnes Russes à la caserne', *Le Miroir*, 19 August 1917.

proof of women's patriotism and of Russia's willingness to continue to participate in the war (despite evidence to the contrary), designed to raise morale and
reassure readers about the combined strength of the Allied Forces. For example,
an article in the British press published in September 1917 stated: 'Slaughter
may not be women's work, but the woman who will sacrifice her womanhood
on the altar of patriotism is a heroine self-evident. ... The energy of Russian
women startles but does not appal. Their vitality has not unsexed them'.[100] This
kind of praise diverged from the private responses of Western diplomats
stationed in Russia, who made their disdain clear in their letters and diaries.
American General William Judson wrote in a letter to his wife in
September 1917: 'I enclose a picture of a Woman's battalion. The Russians
have a lot of them and they are very useless and absurd'.[101] Similarly, Joseph
Noulens, the French Ambassador, wrote in his diary: 'I saw these unfortunates
when they passed under the windows of the French embassy .... They marched
in step, affecting a martial spirit which was obviously contradicted by their
plump figures and their feminine waddle'.[102] These contradictory responses
were particularly evident in the United States, where the mixed reception of the
women soldiers crystallised 'the debate about female citizenship and women's
claims for self-defence' more broadly.[103] While some articles praised the
Russian women's patriotism and sacrifice for the nation, other journalists
questioned their sexual morality, and the *New York Times* stated that their
primary function was 'as an object lesson to the malingerers and peace
mongerers'.[104]

Soviet evocations of Russian women who fought in the First World War
produced in later decades aligned more with criticisms of female combatants as
unwomanly or sexually deviant than with the praise of them as embodying
a noble spirit of French revolutionaries. Karen Petrone notes that there were few
cultural representations of women soldiers in interwar Soviet memories of the
First World War, but that they became a more frequent reference point during
the Second World War, when they were presented as undesirable female models
tainted by their associations with the tsarist war effort. For example, in Sergei
Sergeev-Tsenskii's 1944 novel *Brusilov's Breakthrough*, the hero Livensev is

---

[100] Anon, 'The New Russia', *Reading Observer*, 1 September 1917.

[101] W. V. Judson, *Russia in War and Revolution: General William V. Judson's Accounts from Petrograd, 1917–18* (Kent, OH: Kent State University Press, 1998), p. 89. Quoted in Stockdale, 'My Death for the Motherland', p. 96.

[102] Quoted in R. V. Daniels, *Red October: The Bolshevik Revolution of 1917* (New York: Charles Scribner's Sons, 1967), p. 137.

[103] K. Jensen, *Mobilizing Minerva: American Women in the First World War* (Champaign, IL: University of Illinois Press, 2008), Chapter 4.

[104] *New York Times*, 25 June 1917.

horrified by a female soldier's 'lack of true womanliness', and the character functions, in opposition to Livensev's love interest, a virginal war nurse, as a symbol of everything that was wrong with the tsarist army.[105] Such romanticised Soviet visions of women's wartime roles clashed not only with women's participation in the Civil War, but with the realities of the Second World War, in which over a million women served in the Soviet armed forces and as partisans.[106] As the war progressed, increasing numbers of women carried out combat roles and carried arms, blurring the boundaries between combatant and non-combatant. However, despite the extent of women's militarisation in the 'Great Patriotic War' of 1941–5, the majority of war propaganda posters produced in Russia offered a conservative vision of gender roles. Women were exhorted to step into men's shoes, including for the armed forces, but this was presented as a temporary necessity to save the nation. Their potential as future brides and mothers was constantly emphasised, and a gendered hierarchy remained in place.[107] Thus, Soviet women working for the armed forces, including in combat roles, were represented and heroised according to a traditional hierarchical understanding of men's and women's wartime roles that followed the 'double helix' model as theorised by Margaret and Patrice Higonnet, in which 'the changes in women's activities during wartime did not improve their status' as 'the female strand on the helix is opposed to the male strand, and position on the female strand is subordinate to position on the male strand'.[108] Although the double helix model does not explain more subtle and gradual transformation of the ways in which women's relationships to the military and to the state were changed by their participation in both world wars, it nonetheless offers a helpful way of understanding how any shifts in women's rights and roles in wartime, such as the extensive Soviet use of women in their armed forces, were often understood and presented at the time as temporary transgressions of gender norms that did not threaten women's underlying femininity.

Soviet women were also used for wartime mobilisation in other Allied nations. In Britain, for example, Soviet-style imagery of women patriotically mobilised for war but maintaining their femininity was seen as an essential tool

---

[105] K. Petrone, *The Great War in Russian Memory* (Bloomington, IN: Indiana University Press, 2011), pp. 275–76.

[106] K. J. Cottam, 'Soviet Women in Combat in World War II: The Ground Forces and the Navy', *International Journal of Women's Studies* 3:4 (1980), 345–57.

[107] S. Corbesero, 'Femininity (Con)scripted: Female Images in Soviet Wartime Poster Propaganda, 1941–1945', *Aspasia* 4:1 (2010), 103–20 (p. 107).

[108] P. Higonnet and M. R. Higonnet, 'The Double Helix', in M. R. Higonnet, J. Jenson, S. Michel and M. Collins Weitz (eds.), *Behind the Lines: Gender and the Two World Wars* (New Haven, CT: Yale University Press, 1987), pp. 31–49 (p. 34).

in the government's need to swell the wartime workforce: 'In British propaganda and popular culture, the Soviet woman . . . reconciled labour with domestic responsibility, maintained her good looks without succumbing to vanity, and embraced militancy without compromising women's peacemaking and nurturing qualities'.[109] As a result, many British Second World War posters either directly or indirectly referenced Soviet women. However, this kind of discourse was more difficult to maintain in relation to female frontline combatants in the Russian armed forces, who were being celebrated for taking rather than giving life. Jean Knox, Director of the British Auxiliary Territorial Service (ATS) from 1941 to 1943, was keen to differentiate British women's non-combatant war roles from those of Soviet combatant women:

> Women have won a merited place in the active army, but they cannot be trained to kill. I don't believe women can take life as men can. I know nothing of Russia, but I know women. Women give life. They are not designed to take life, even in total war.[110]

This ambivalent attitude towards Soviet women soldiers in the Second World War is equally illustrated in the Allied representation and reception of sniper Lyudmila Pavlichenko, who became a global media star. Before the war, Pavlichenko had been a history student at the University of Kyiv and paramilitary activist who already had some experience of shooting. She volunteered in summer 1941, and within a year allegedly had 309 kills to her name. Her achievements were first publicised in the Soviet Union by male combatants, including a Sergeant Grigorov who sent a sketch of her to *Komsomolskaia Pravda*, the official organ of the youth wing of the Communist Party of the Soviet Union, from besieged Sebastopol. Her fame spread quickly, and she was regularly featured as a heroic 'sniper girl' in the Soviet press. Like Bochkareva before her, Pavlichenko was a willing participant in her mediatisation, writing articles and giving rousing speeches at rallies. Anna Krylova argues that the positive public reception of Soviet female soldiers and pilots in the Second World War led to a desire to repeatedly display their military prowess to their male supervisors: 'the male gaze was . . . treated by young women pilots, snipers, and commanders as a prompt for self-display in combat'.[111] In Pavlichenko's case, her high success rate as a sniper was a key ingredient in

[109] C. Ward, '"Something of the Spirit of Stalingrad": British Women, Their Soviet Sisters, Propaganda and Politics in the Second World War', *Twentieth Century British History* 25:3 (2014), 435–60 (p. 436).

[110] Anon, 'Women Are Not Killers – ATS Chief', *Courier and Advertiser*, 1 October 1942. Quoted in Crang, *Sisters in Army*, pp. 69–70.

[111] A. Krylova, *Soviet Women in Combat: A History of Violence on the Eastern Front* (Cambridge: Cambridge University Press, 2010), p. 242

Figure 7 'Female sniper Lyudmila Pavlichenko in a trench', *Smema Magazine* 12 (1942)

her media profile as a war heroine (Figure 7). In late 1942, she was selected by the Young Communist League and Stalinist government to go on a tour of Britain, the United States, and Canada with three male comrades as a 'role model of an active-duty, successful and confident female combatant'.[112] Her heroisation as a glamorous young 'sniper girl' continued in the British, American, and Canadian press. Articles which featured her exploits had the primary aim of mobilising civilian women into a range of non-combatant wartime roles, as did the numerous invitations to speak at rallies and public events. Pavlichenko and her colleagues toured factories, warehouses, and dockyards, and spoke of their admiration of civilians' contributions to the war effort on behalf of the Soviet people.[113] Her story appealed to wartime populations, and she attracted large crowds.[114] Journalists expressed their fascination for the 'unlikely' combination of her glamorous, feminine appearance, and ruthless efficiency as a sniper: one caption beneath a photograph of her aiming her gun described her as 'The Girl with Deadly Aim and a Dimple'.[115] At the

---

[112] Ibid., p. 159.

[113] In November 1942, for example, Pavlichenko 'thanked the people of Liverpool from the people of the Soviet Union' after touring shipyards, a factory, and the University of Liverpool. Anon, 'Pavlichenko's Tribute to City', *Liverpool Evening Express*, 24 November 1942.

[114] D. Gucciardo and M. Howatt, 'Sniper Girls and Fearless Heroines: Wartime Representations of Foreign Women in English-Canadian Press, 1941–1943', in B. Hacker and M. Vining (eds.), *A Companion to Women's Military History* (Leiden: Brill, 2012), pp. 547–67.

[115] Anon, 'Forty Eight Women Against Hitler', *Daily News*, 7 November 1942.

same time, they continually and firmly emphasised the fact that other Allied women's contributions to the war effort should be in non-combatant roles.

As had been the case in the First World War, journalists and other commentators argued that while women like Pavlichenko should be lauded for their bravery and patriotic devotion, these sentiments should be channelled into more gender-appropriate activity in the case of non-Soviet Allied women's war contributions. Thus, Russian/Soviet women in both world wars were depicted in contradictory ways in foreign press coverage. In the Second World War Canadian press, for example, the representation of Soviet women soldiers was aligned with that of Chinese guerrilla fighters as 'battle-weary and tough', in contrast to Canadian servicewomen who were 'portrayed through images of heightened femininity and womanliness'.[116] In the world wars, Russian/Soviet women warriors were used to mobilise Allied men and women into the war effort, but there were clear limits to their function as direct role models for other women in nations where the idea of women in frontline combat roles remained taboo. In order to differentiate between Russian/Soviet and other Allied women, reporters regularly resorted to ethnographic stereotypes, emphasising Russian/Soviet women's 'hardy', 'brave', or 'virile' nature, and categorising the societies to which they belonged as 'backward' or 'uncivilised' in relation to the West. More critical portrayals attacked them for straying from the norms of chaste Joan-of-Arc-like heroism, and hinted at either lesbianism or promiscuity in their sexual behaviours.[117] In contrast, other Allied women continued to be portrayed in traditional ways as support workers for militarised men who maintained their femininity and concomitant potential to give birth to future citizen-soldiers. Despite the reality of thousands of women performing frontline combat roles in the world wars, in Soviet recruitment propaganda that lauded motherhood as women's primary national duty, and in Allied receptions of Russian women soldiers, attempts were repeatedly made to retrace the boundaries of traditional gender norms in relation to the changes to men's and women's wartime lives. In other words, Cynthia Enloe's definition of militarisation in which 'the inner sanctum [of] combat' is inherently bound up with concepts of masculinity and national identity was still very much in evidence.

3 Women Warriors as Icons of Resistance

The previous section argued that female soldiers were often used in the world wars as a means of mobilising wartime populations in ways that did not radically challenge gender norms, even if their very existence clearly brought into question essentialist claims about women's innate unsuitability for combat.

---

[116] Gucciardo and Howatt, 'Sniper Girls', pp. 563–64.   [117] Jensen, *Mobilizing Minerva*, p. 70.

In this section, I examine women warrior figures who were presented as more threatening to the status quo. This was particularly the case with the women warriors who were evoked as a means of mobilising support for resistance movements, whether such movements were resisting occupation by a foreign power, colonialism or imperialism, or patriarchal societies that curtailed women's rights and roles. During periods of resistance, anti-resistance discourse demonised resistant women warriors, presenting them 'either as … radical and hyper-sexualised or even deviant figure[s], or as unnatural and inhuman genderless aberration[s]'.[118] If resistance movements led to liberation, decolonisation or independence, however, some of these women were subsequently re-invoked and re-imagined as national heroines. This was the case with African women warriors Mekatilili wa Meza, Yaa Asantewaa, and Lalla Fatma N'Soumer. During the Giriama uprising of 1913 and 1914 in Kenya, Mekatilili wa Meza was described by British colonial officials as 'a half-mad woman' who 'tours the country preaching active opposition to Government' and as a 'witch'.[119] Her story was re-discovered by post-independence generations, however, and more recently she has been presented in Kenya as a feminist icon and national heroine. In 2010, festivals were organised to celebrate her story, and the National Museums of Kenya recently produced an animated version of her life entitled 'The Story of the Giriama Wonder Woman', depicting her as 'one of Kenya's earliest freedom fighters'.[120] Similarly, as Naaborko Sackeyfio-Lenoch notes, 'interpretations of Yaa Asantewaa's position shifted over the course of the twentieth century from political prisoner, dangerous subversive, and anti-colonial leader to having schools named in her honor'.[121] In 2000, a series of centenary commemorative activities celebrated her role in the 1901 war against the British, and a museum dedicated to her was opened in Ejisu. Finally, Lalla Fatma N'Soumer, a prophetess who mobilised and commanded the armed Kabyle resistance movement against French colonists in the 1850s, and who was depicted in nineteenth-century French Orientalist art and writing such as the 1866 painting of her by Félix Philippoteaux on horseback leading the armed resistance alongside Chérif Boubaghla, has been celebrated in recent years as a national heroine in Algeria. In addition to a 2014 film,

---

[118] Cothran, Judge and Shubert, 'Introduction', p. 3.

[119] N. Carrier and C. Nyamweru, 'Reinventing Africa's National Heroes: The Case of Mekatilili, a Kenyan Popular Heroine', *African Affairs*, 115:461 (2016), 599–620, https://doi.org/10.1093/afraf/adw051

[120] National Museums of Kenya, 'Mekatilili Wa Menza: The Story of the Giriama Wonder Woman', https://artsandculture.google.com/story/mekatilili-wa-menza-the-story-of-the-giriama-wonder-woman/uQJiyBBzmBOAKg.

[121] Sackeyfio-Lenoch, 'Reframing Yaa Asantewaa', pp. 140–1.

Fathma N'Soumer, several schools and streets are named after her, and statues erected to her memory in Algiers and Tizi-Ldjama.[122]

3.1 The Rani of Jhansi

The Rani of Jhansi is another example of a woman warrior figure whose long and complicated cultural afterlives follow the pattern of demonisation followed by a series of 're-discoveries' of her as a warrior-heroine by nationalist and anti-colonial movements. Lakshmi Bai (née Manikarnika) fought against the British in the First War of Independence in India, and was the widow of the Maharaja Gangadhar Rao, who died in 1853, earning her the title of Rani. Following the revolt against British rule in 1857, in which the town of Jhansi was besieged, she joined other rebel forces to defend the town, allegedly on horseback and wearing male clothing. She was eventually killed on the battlefield near Gwalior, and in the decades following her death became a figure of fascination both within and beyond India, inspiring a spate of novels, poems, plays, statues, songs, films, and television dramas.[123]

Harleen Singh's detailed study of cultural and political representations of the Rani of Jhansi reveals her popularity as a figure in British Orientalist writings throughout the nineteenth and twentieth centuries. British portrayals of her ranged from praise of her courage as the 'Indian Joan of Arc' to damning indictments of her 'deviant' sexuality. These responses not only mirrored the usual ways in which armed women were represented in this period but also embodied the contradictions to be found at the heart of British imperial policy, in which Indian women were frequently positioned in colonial and orientalist discourse as vulnerable women to be protected and rescued from oppression. Thus, as Singh notes:

> As an Indian woman relegated to a life of purdah, the Rani may have garnered sympathy, but as an Indian Queen who came out of the veil in rebellion against the British, she posed an interminable problem of representation and comprehension. As an Indian widow who had become sati or shaved her head and dedicated herself to a life of hardship, she may have excited a chivalric response, but as a royal widow who commanded troops and took British lives, she defied both rescue and reform.[124]

---

[122] P. Philippoteaux, 'Portraits of Chérif Boubaghla and Lalla Fatma N'Soumer leading the revolutionary army', 1866; S. Touati, 'Lalla Fatma N'Soumer (1830–1863): Spirituality, Resistance and Womanly Leadership in Colonial Algeria', *Societies* 8:4 (2018), 1–16.

[123] On the numerous Indian ballads, poems, novels, films, and television dramas featuring the Rani of Jhansi, see P. Maurya and N. Kumar, 'Manikarnika: The Queen of Jhansi and its Topicality', *South Asian Popular Culture*, 18:3 (2020), 247–260, https://doi.org/10.1080/14746689 .2020.1815452.

[124] H. Singh, *The Rani of Jhansi: Gender, History and Fable in India* (Cambridge: Cambridge University Press, 2014), p. 18.

This political context explains the frequently contradictory and ambiguous representations of the Rani of Jhansi produced by British writers and journalists. Some accounts presented her aggressively sexually pursuing British men, thereby positioning her as a *femme fatale*, the negative other of a chaste warrior-heroine. In contrast, other re-tellings of her story overtly aligned her to Joan of Arc, such as Michael White's 1901 novel *Lachmi Bai Rani of Jhansi: The Jeanne D'Arc of India* (Figure 8). In this novel, her difference from other Indian women is emphasised:

> Lachmi Bai, Rani of Jhansi, was far removed from the generally accepted type of her countrywomen. . . . [T]here was a strength of character emphasized in every line of her distinctly Aryan features, a force of will, a mystical power in every flash of her lustrous eyes, in every movement, in every word, however gently spoken, warning him at the outset that he had to deal with no shrinking, simple, *zanana* maiden.[125]

White thereby 'whitewashes' his protagonist, retaining a sense of her 'exotic' feminine appeal while aligning her with a Western model of female armed heroism and distancing her from negative representations of resistant Indians. The tradition of comparing Lakshmi Bai to Joan of Arc in an attempt to offer a positive colonial vision of British-Indian relations continued amongst British writers into the twentieth century. In a Foreword to his 1933 play *Rani of Jhansi*, for example, playwright Philip Cox wrote: 'No one who studies the very meagre evidence that is available concerning this remarkable woman can help being struck by resemblances between the chequered life of the Rani and the reputed career of the Maid of Orleans'. Cox expressed the wish that rather than provoking nationalist resistance to British rule, 'a sympathetic portrait of the Indian counterpart of Joan of Arc may do something to bridge the gulf of ignorance and prejudice that separates Britain and India'.[126] In reality, however, his portrayal of a love affair between the Rani and a British officer in his play provoked widespread protest in India.[127]

Amongst Indian artists, poets, and writers, the Rani of Jhansi became a potent and popular symbol of resistance. She was evoked as a role model in different traditions of Indian nationalism, but especially by nationalists seeking to promote an alternative to Gandhian non-violent revolution. Shortly after her death, she was immortalised in songs and ballads, and paintings of her adorned shrines in Indian temples and homes, in which she was usually identified with Hindu goddesses. In these images, she was depicted in warrior mode on horseback,

---

[125] White, *Laskhmi Bai*, p. 12.
[126] P. Cox, *The Rani of Jhansi: A Historical Play in Four Acts* (London: Heinemann, 1933)
[127] Singh, *The Rani of Jhansi*, p. 142.

Her horse leaped forward, straight for Sindhia's guns.—Page 255.

Figure 8 'Her horse leaped forward, straight for Sindhia's guns'. Illustration in Michael White, *Lachmi Bai Rani of Jhansi: The Jeanne d'Arc of India* (1901)

half-Queen, half-deity. As Joyce Lebra-Chapman notes, 'the Rani's wearing of male battle regalia is related to the theme of Hindu deity as androgyne', therefore representing her as a Hindu goddess protected her from potential accusations that a woman had transgressed her 'natural' duties by usurping a male military role.[128] As is the case with other mythical female warrior

---

[128] J. Lebra-Chapman, *Rani of Jhansi: A Study in Female Heroism in India* (Honolulu, HI: University of Hawaii Press, 1986), p. 124.

figures, in these images her powers remain situated firmly in the realm of the symbolic, and do not pose a threat to the patriarchal status quo.

In the 1920s and 1930s, images of the Rani of Jhansi continued to be used as a call to resistance by Indian nationalists both within and beyond India. The front cover of the May 1926 issue of *The United States of India*, the journal of the pro-independence Pacific Coast Hindustani Association (which was later renamed the Ghadar Party), for example, featured a drawing of the Rani in male clothing brandishing a sword, and described her as the 'Heroine of the War of Independence of 1857'.[129] Following the marking of her grave in Gwalior by the Archaeological Survey in 1929, Indian poet Krishna Baldev Verma published an article praising the Rani in the nationalist newspaper *Vishal Bharat*, which was immediately banned.[130] One of the best-known twentieth-century literary portraits was the Hindi poem 'The Rani of Jhansi' by Subhadra Kumari Chauhan, first published in 1930, and which after independence became a staple of school and college curricula and was inscribed on a stone table at the entrance to the Fort of Jhansi.[131] Nehru described her in his 1934 memoir written in prison as 'the one bright spot against [the] dark background' of 1857, as a 'girl-widow, twenty years of age, who donned a man's dress and came out to lead her people against the British'.[132] Finally, in Mulk Raj Anand's 1939 novel *Across the Black Waters*, which tells the story of Indian participation in the First World War, the Rani is once again compared to Joan of Arc, but this time as a critique rather than as a justification of colonial rule:

> Lalu rushed up, and craned his neck to see the figure of a young girl with a sword in her hand, her head thrust heroically forward, and her whole body speaking of some brave deed which she had performed. 'Jean d'Arc' the inscription at the foot of the statue said. In a flash the last clue to Orleans returned to his memory from the story of *Joan of Arc* in the *Highroads of History* that he'd read at the Church Mission School. ... And the maid seemed to become a heroine like the Rani of Jhansi. Lalu felt the blood cursing in his veins with the ambition to follow her on the path of glory.[133]

Here, Anand uses the encounter of Indian sepoys with a statue of Joan of Arc in France to unmask the ways in which his education led the protagonist, Lalu, to internalise colonial models of military heroism. Whereas at this point in the

---

[129] SADDA, Ghadar Party Collection, www.saada.org/item/20111129-508.

[130] Lebra-Chapman, *Rani of Jhansi*, p. 145.

[131] V. Chauhan, 'Lakshmibai and Jhalkaribai: Women Heroes and Contesting Caste and Gender Paradigms and Histories', *South Asian Review* 37:2 (2016), 81–98, https://doi.org/10.1080/02759527.2016.11933063.

[132] J. Nehru, *Glimpses of World History* (Bombay: Asia Publishing House,1967), p. 428. Quoted in Shubert, 'Women Warriors and National Heroes', p. 284.

[133] M. Anand, *Across the Black Waters* (New Delhi: Orient Paperbacks, 2008), p. 34.

narrative, as Santanu Das notes, 'imperial war and nationalist resistance get conflated in the excitement of military service', Lalu gradually comes to view the British use of Indian troops as another form of colonial exploitation.[134] For the novel's readers, this scene underscores the dramatic irony of the protagonist's evocation of Joan of Arc and the Rani of Jhansi, both leaders of violent uprisings against British power, as vehicles for mobilising Indian troops to risk their lives for the British Empire.

Nationalist interpretations of the Rani's story generally included details that firmly placed her within traditional gender codes, such as the popular depiction of her as a warrior with her child tied to her back.[135] This combination of sword-wielding resistance heroine and mother is a familiar trope in cultural evocations of warrior women during this period, and constitutes an attempt to neutralise the warriors' potential to challenge the primacy of motherhood in models of female identity. The trope is also present, for example, in depictions of Nene Hatun, a Turkish heroine of the Turkish-Russian War (1877–8). When Nene Hatun participated in the armed defence of the Aziziye Bastions at Erzurum against Russian forces, taking up the rifle of her brother who had been wounded, she was a twenty-year-old mother with a three-month-old son. She was originally only remembered in Erzurum, but in the 1930s her story appeared in the national press, and in the anti-Soviet mood in Turkey following the Second World War her identity as an iconic woman warrior gained further traction, particularly when she was visited in 1952 by US General Matthew Bunker Ridgway, NATO Supreme Commander of the Allied Forces, which helped to propagate her story. In 1955 she was named 'Mother of the Year' by the Turkish Women's Union. More recently, in 1998, a statue was erected (Figure 9) depicting her triumphantly holding her rifle aloft with her baby strapped to her back. Her twentieth-century incarnation as 'the Mother of Mothers' of the Turkish nation, in which her military defence of her homeland is seen as a natural extension of her maternal nurturing of her child, is reminiscent of many nationalist depictions of the Rani of Jhansi.[136] As Cynthia Enloe argues in her analysis of a photograph of a Spanish Civil War *miliciana* holding her baby, 'interweaving the images of woman as combatant and mother so tightly suggests that as soon as the immediate threat recedes, as soon as the "war is over", the woman in the picture will put down the rifle and keep the baby'.[137]

---

[134] S. Das, *India, Empire and First World War Culture* (Cambridge: Cambridge University Press, 2018), p. 357.

[135] Chauhan, 'Lakshmibai and Jhalkaribai', p. 91.

[136] G. Emen-Gökatalay, 'Popularising and Promoting Nene Hatun as an Iconic Turkish Mother in Early Cold War Turkey', *Journal of Middle East Women's Studies* 17:1 (2021), 43–63, https://doi.org/10.1215/15525864-8790224.

[137] Enloe, *Does Khaki Become You?*, p. 166.

Figure 9 Metin Yurdanur, 'Nene Hatun', Erzurum, Turkey, 1998. Photograph by Eğitmen Mahmut

Even in post-independence India, when nationalist writers and poets were able to write freely about 1857, portraits of the Rani of Jhansi tended not to transgress gender norms. However, not all re-tellings of her story represented her as a mythical warrior-goddess-mother rather than as an armed role model for twentieth-century Indian women to emulate. On 14 August 1945, the Rani of Jhansi was again the central character in a play, this time performed in Singapore by the Indian women of the Rani of Jhansi Regiment, which had been founded by nationalist leader Subhas Chandra Bose two years earlier.[138]

---

[138] G. Forbes, 'Mothers and Sisters: Feminism and Nationalism in the Thought of Subhas Chandra Bose', *Asian Studies* 2:1 (1984), 23–32 (p. 30).

Around 1,500 women in Burma, Malaya, and Singapore enlisted in the Regiment as part of Bose's attempts to mobilise Indian communities in South East Asia for the liberation of India. Bose's nationalism in the 1920s and 1930s had been marked by a relatively progressive vision of women's rights and roles, as he sought to abolish child marriage, purdah, and the prohibition on the remarriage of widows, and promoted female education and economic independence.[139] In 1941, he escaped house arrest and travelled to Nazi Germany, where he organised 4,500 Indian POWs who had previously fought for the British in North Africa into an Indian Legion, supported by Nazi authorities. However, after becoming disillusioned by Hitler's invasion of the Soviet Union he was transferred via German and Japanese submarines to South East Asia, and there attempted to revive an Indian National Army. His choice of the Rani of Jhansi as the name of his 'unit of brave Indian women' can be seen as a 'safe' choice, given her high profile in nationalist circles on the one hand, and the extent to which the majority of Indian cultural representations enfolded her within traditional feminine and/or religious models of female identity on the other.[140] The narrator of *Jai-Hind*, an anonymously published diary of a member of the Regiment, claims to have first heard Bose on the Berlin Radio in April 1942, and describes how 'thrilled' she was by his nationalist rhetoric, before he arrived in Singapore and directly called for female recruits to form a 'death-defying regiment, which wields the sword which the Rani of Jhansi wielded'.[141] Bose's recruitment efforts were aided by the Regiment's leader, Dr Lakshmi Swaminadhan, an obstetrician and nationalist activist based in Singapore who helped to persuade Indian women and their families of the respectability and urgency of the cause. *Jai-Hind*, which like other published memoirs by former members offers an overwhelmingly positive assessment of the motivations and actions of Bose's nationalist Azad Hind movement, suggests that the women soldiers were keen to live up to the ideals of heroic militarised womanhood that the regiment embodied:

> With rifles in our hands, we listened to [Bose's] speech, standing like statues, not daring to breathe lest we create an unfavourable impression on him about our capacity to become active soldiers in the field of battle. I tremble at the new life that is opening out before me. I pray that I should never be found wanting – never – never for an instant let weakness make me bend.[142]

---

[139] C. Hills and D. C. Silverman, 'Nationalism and Feminism in Late Colonial India: The Rani of Jhansi Regiment', *Modern Asian Studies* 27:4 (1993), 741–60 (p. 753).

[140] T. F. Rettig, 'Recruiting the All Female Rani of Jhansi Regiment: Subhas Chandra Bose and Dr Lakshmi Swaminadhan', *South East Asia Research* 21:4 (2013), 627–38 (p. 630).

[141] Anon, *Jai-Hind: The Diary of a Rebel Daughter of India with the Rani of Jhansi Regiment* (Bombay: Janmabhoomi Prakashan Mandir, 1945).

[142] Ibid., p. 67.

In reality, however, the Regiment's actions did not lead to any military or tactical successes. After training, the women were deployed to Burma from March 1944 to August 1945. When the British advanced, they were forced to retreat, and after the surrender of Rangoon to the British, veterans were repatriated to their homes in Burma, Malaya, and Singapore, and Dr Lakshmi Swaminadhan returned to India.[143] Bose died when the Japanese plane he was travelling in crashed on 18 August. The performance of the play on 14 August, then, was the final dramatisation of the Regiment's members 'wielding the sword' of the Rani.

The use of the Rani of Jhansi as a mobilising figure for Indian female combatants resonates strongly with two other groups of female combatants in the Second World War who were named after nineteenth-century women warriors. In Greece, the 'Bouboulina group', an underground resistance organisation in Axis-occupied Greece, was named after Laskarina Bouboulina, a military leader in the Greek War of Independence in 1821.[144] The Bouboulina group was founded by Lela Karayanni (or Karagianni) in May 1941, and initially helped Allied soldiers flee to the Middle East, before becoming associated with the wider intelligence network of resistance groups in Greece. Karayanni was betrayed and arrested on 11 July 1944, and was executed on 8 September 1944 at the Haidari camp in Athens.[145] Greek writings on and cultural representations of Karayanni produced since the end of the Second World War have tended to present her, like her group's namesake, as a remarkable and singular national heroine, 'on the one hand ... as a Superwoman of the Resistance who ran her own group and planned her activities without any assistance, and on the other hand ... as a devoted housewife of impeccable middle-class credentials, devoted to the family values of twentieth-century Greece'. In reality, Karayanni was one of many Greek 'soldier[s] in the secret army who had to follow orders' of British intelligence organisations, but her status as a national Greek war heroine has been aided by her association with Bouboulina.[146] The Emilia Plater Regiment was founded in 1943 as an all-female unit of the Soviet Polish Army, and was largely made up of Polish deportees from occupied eastern Poland in 1940 and 1941, alongside Soviet and Polish communists. Members were called 'Platerówki', and numbered up to 8,000 in total. When they entered Polish territory alongside the Red Army in 1944, they were received 'with a mixture of pity and awe', which is

---

[143] J. Lebra, *Women Against the Raj: The Rani of Jhansi Regiment* (Singapore: Institute of South East Asian Studies, 2008), Chapter 8.

[144] Pennington (ed.), *Amazons to Fighter Pilots*, Vol 1, p. 65; Toler, *Women Warriors*, p. 128.

[145] S. Perrakis, *The Improbable Heroine: Lela Karayanni and the British Secret Services in World War II Greece* (Berlin: De Gruyter, 2022).

[146] Ibid., p. 8.

reminiscent of responses to the Rani of Jhansi Regiment as described in the memoirs of former members.[147] While the political contexts in which these three groups of women soldiers in the Second World War were formed differed, their names reveal the extent to which nineteenth-century female warriors had the power to mobilise women into military roles in the mid-twentieth century. The Rani of Jhansi, Bouboulina and Plater not only acted as role models of bravery and patriotism for female recruits, but crucially gave their armed war service respectability, enshrining it within national identity myths that protected them, at least in part, from gender-based criticisms as women who were taking up frontline combat roles.

3.2 Women Warriors and Women's Rights Campaigns

Another key use of armed women as inspiring role models in the early to mid-twentieth century, and one that offered a more disruptive vision of women warriors in terms of traditional gender roles, was in feminist and suffrage campaigns. Pageants and parades were a key strategy deployed by European and North American first-wave feminist movements, and regularly featured suffragist activists dressed as inspirational resistant women from the past. Given her widespread fame, it is unsurprising that Joan of Arc was the most popular choice. Different tendencies within the suffrage movement emphasised different aspects of her myth in order to rally their supporters and broaden their movement's appeal to new audiences. For some suffrage activists, Joan was depicted as a triumphant military leader, leading her troops to victory, while others emphasised the Catholic vision of her as a saintly martyr, called to fulfil a righteous mission. Both these versions were discernible in early twentieth-century suffrage representations of Joan of Arc.

In June 1913, British suffragette Emily Wilding Davison laid a wreath at the foot of a statue of Joan of Arc at the Women's Social and Political Union (WSPU) Summer Fair and Fete in Kensington the day before she was killed stepping in front of the King's horse at the Epsom Derby.[148] Davison's spectacular funeral procession included fellow WSPU member Emily Howey dressed as Joan of Arc on horseback, and banners in purple silk printed with Joan's alleged final words 'Fight on and God will give the Victory'.[149] This was

---

[147] M. Fidelis, *Women, Communism and Industrialisation in Postwar Poland* (Cambridge: Cambridge University Press, 2013), p. 38.

[148] The Museum of London contains a photograph of this statue of Joan of Arc, sword held aloft, with a wreath stating 'In Honour and in Loving and Revered Memory of Emily Wilding Davison. She Died for Women'. Museum of London, postcard with a photograph of a statue of Joan of Arc, H. Serjeant, 1913, 50.82/923c.

[149] Museum of London, 'That malignant suffragette: Remembering Emily Davison', www.museumoflondon.org.uk/discover/malignant-suffragette-remembering-emily-wilding-davison.

not the first time Howey had performed the role: Joan of Arc was a staple of suffrage parades, both in Britain and in the United States, where the role of suffrage herald mirrored the British suffrage visions of Joan, 'representing moral authority and righteousness for the cause'.[150] In American parades, pacifist feminist Inez Milholland performed this role astride a white horse, and her appearances were much commented upon by journalists. Interpreting Joan of Arc through the lens of the New Woman and the popular revival of medievalism, Howey and Milholland embodied an alternative model of female identity, and did so in spectacular fashion. The press 'lapped up the medieval spectacle of banners, floats and bands', helping to bring the 'mass media exposure that transformed the cause into a mass movement'.[151] When Milholland died in 1916, her casting as Joan of Arc continued to be foregrounded in the suffrage press and she was presented as a martyr of the American suffrage movement.

In the British movement, Christabel Pankhurst described Joan of Arc in her autobiography as the spiritual foremother of the suffragettes, and claimed her as the movement's patron saint.[152] Christabel Pankhurst, alongside her mother Emmeline, was comfortable with a militarist version of Joan of Arc as a model of feminist resistance. This is evidenced after the outbreak of the First World War when Joan was featured in martial mode on the front cover of WSPU journal *The Suffragette* in May 1915 as 'The Great Patriot', reproducing Jean-Auguste-Dominique Ingrès's painting 'Joan of Arc at the Coronation of King Charles VII' (1854), and thereby realigning her as a symbol of both the movement and the Allied war effort.[153] In contrast, the Catholic Women's Suffrage Society, founded as a constitutional non-militant suffrage organisation, and renamed St Joan's Social and Political Alliance in 1923, carried an embroidered banner in suffrage processions featuring Joan of Arc alongside the words 'Jesus' and 'Marie', emphasising the religious elements of her persona.[154] These examples demonstrate how the varied depictions of Joan of Arc in suffrage material showcased different conceptions of women's active citizenship and a range of opinions amongst activists about what forms

---

[150] J. L. Borda, 'The Woman Suffrage Parades of 1910–1913: Possibilities and Limitations of an Early Feminist Rhetorical Strategy', *Western Journal of Communication* (2002), 66:1, 25–52, https://doi.org/10.1080/10570310209374724 (p. 38).

[151] L. J. Lumsden, *Inez: The Life and Times of Inez Milholland* (Bloomington, IN: Indiana University Press, 2008), p. 70.

[152] L. E. Nym Mayhall, *The Militant Suffrage Movement: Citizenship and Resistance in Britain, 1860–1930* (Oxford: Oxford University Press, 2003), p. 87.

[153] Front cover, *The Suffragette*, 14 May 1915.

[154] E. Crawford, blog, 'Suffrage Stories: Is This Edith Craig's Banner for the Catholic Women's Suffrage Society?', https://womanandhersphere.com/2019/02/26/suffrage-stories-is-this-edith-craigs-banner-for-the-catholic-womens-suffrage-society/.

resistance to the state should take, including disagreements about the role of violence. The malleability of Joan of Arc as a warrior-heroine or martyr-saint meant that she could be adopted by both militarist and pacifist feminists. However, neither feminist vision of Joan necessarily tallied with broader cultural understandings of her myth. In Britain this was illustrated in December 1913, when a performance of Raymond Roze's opera *Joan of Arc*, which was attended by the King and Queen, was disrupted by three WSPU members who used a megaphone to proclaim to the Royal Box 'We wish to draw an analogy between the opera your majesties are witnessing and ... the policy of persecution adopted towards women fighting for a principle and an ideal for liberty'. Press reports attest that their cries were greeted with calls of 'Sit down' and 'Throw them out' from a 'wholly unsympathetic' audience, revealing the limitations of their attempts to co-opt Joan of Arc to their cause among the wider public.[155]

The tensions at play in the uses of Joan of Arc to represent the diverse strands of early twentieth-century feminism, whether radical or moderate, pacifist or militarist, religious or secular, were not only evident in the West. Joan of Arc also appeared as a model of female identity in the Chinese women's press in the early decades of the twentieth century. Collections of life stories of 'Famous Women', or what Alison Booth terms 'collective biography' or 'prosopography', had been a popular genre across the globe for centuries, and served didactic and nationalist functions.[156] Chinese examples in the late nineteenth and early twentieth centuries, such as female poet and educator Xue Shaohui's *Biographies of Foreign Women*, often included Joan of Arc. They were influenced by the 1898 Reform Movement, which was triggered by China's defeat in the 1894–5 Sino-Japanese war, leading elite Chinese men and women to turn to the West for models of reform, including exemplars of virtuous womanhood.[157] Chinese collections were also influenced by the popular trend for women's 'self-help' literature in Japan in the Meiji period. While some of the Chinese portraits of Joan of Arc underscored traditional understandings of women's identities, others offered a more critical view of the status quo, and presented Joan as a radical example of active citizenship for women. For example, the *Magazine of the New Women's World of China*, which was published in Japan

---

[155] Anon, 'Impressive Protest at the Opera', *The Suffragette*, 19 December 1913; Anon, 'Suffragettes at the Opera', *Western Gazette*, 19 December 1913.

[156] A. Booth, *How to Make It as a Woman: Collective Biographical History from Victoria to the Present* (Chicago, IL: University of Chicago Press, 2004).

[157] N. Qian, 'Competing Conceptualisations of Guo (Country, State and/or Nation State) in Late Qing Women's Journals', in M. Hockx, J. Judge and B. Mittler (eds.), *Women and the Periodical Press in China's Long Twentieth Century* (Cambridge: Cambridge University Press, 2018), pp. 217–35 (p. 226).

from 1907 by Yan Bin, a medical student and member of the Society of Chinese Female Students, aimed to create a 'female citizenry' and included Joan of Arc as one of its Euro-American models for its readers.[158] Mei Zhu, the biography's author, claimed that in contrast to Hua Mulan, who was famous for and motivated by her devotion to her father, Joan was the more impressive warrior as her devotion was to France and its survival.[159] In this way, the journal uses the figure of Joan of Arc to promote Chinese women's potential to take up public and political roles for their nation, rather than being confined to familial duty.

Joan of Arc also regularly appeared as an inspirational example of heroic womanhood in the women's press in Egypt in the same period. Marilyn Booth notes that in published collections of biographies of 'Great Women', Joan of Arc was a more frequent point of reference for the Egyptian women's movement than African or Arabic mythical warrior women such as Khawla bint al-Azwar.[160] Once again, Joan symbolised different political and ideological positions depending on how and why her image was deployed by Egyptian activists:

> [Joan of Arc] could represent the anti-imperialist activist in the service of a nation in formation; the devout believer who puts personal faith into action on behalf of the nation; the peasant as crucial in the national struggle; the young woman as having to reconcile duty to nation with duty to family.[161]

The biographies of Joan that appeared in the Egyptian women's press targeted a readership of elite educated women, including the members of the Egyptian Feminist Union, founded in 1923 and affiliated to the International Women's Suffrage Alliance. Egyptian nationalist feminists were therefore operating within an international context, and were influenced by the feminist interpretations of Joan common in Europe and the United States. However, in what is one of many examples of the 'travelling memory' of Joan of Arc in the nineteenth and twentieth centuries, the biographies that appeared in the Egyptian women's press were equally shaped by emerging anti-colonial thought.[162] Thus, while Joan of Arc appeared across the world as a 'timeless' heroine in didactic literature aimed at providing appropriate role models for

---

[158] X. Xiaohong, 'Heroines in Late Qing Women's Journals: Meiji-Era Writing on "Women's Self-Help"', in Ibid., pp. 236–54.

[159] Y. Zhang, *Engendering the Woman Question: Men, Women and Writing in China's Early Periodical Press* (Leiden: Brill, 2020), pp. 68–69.

[160] M. Booth, 'The Egyptian Lives of Jeanne d'Arc', in L. Abu-Lughod (ed.), *Remaking Women: Feminism and Modernity in the Middle East* (Princeton, NJ: Princeton University Press, 1998), pp. 171–214.

[161] Ibid, p. 172.

[162] Joan of Arc was also presented to educated Hindu women as a heroic model to emulate, for example in 1913 in the Hindu women's periodical *Grihalakshmi*. S. Nijhawan, *Women and Girls in the Hindu Public Sphere* (Oxford: Oxford University Press, 2011).

young women to emulate, in 1920s Egyptian women's journals she was featured 'in full nationalist garb bedecked with dazzling anti-British trimmings'. For example, in the third issue of the journal *Young Women of Young Egypt*, Zaynab Sadiq evokes in her depiction of Joan's English enemies the 'plunder and pillage' of British colonists.[163] The adaptability of Joan of Arc as a woman warrior meant she could be used in colonial and anti-colonial contexts, representing the 'soul' of France in Catholic imperial right-wing publications on the one hand, and functioning in a newly independent Egypt as a 'perfect 1920s . . . female patriot and representative of the nation' on the other.[164]

Joan of Arc was also made to embody anti-British sentiments in performances by Constance Markievicz, who as a member of Irish paramilitary organisations and central figure in the Irish Republican movement frequently played on her persona as a woman warrior in her political activism. Markievicz linked nationalism and feminism, presenting women as the victims of both colonial and patriarchal domination, and condoning the necessity of violence in opposition to both.[165] In a speech to the Students' National Literary Society delivered in Dublin in 1909 entitled 'Women, Ideals and the Nation', Markievicz evoked the 'magnificent legacy of Maeve, Fleas, Macha and other great fighting ancestors' in her call to arms to twentieth-century Irish women, extolling them to 'dress suitably in short skirts and strong boots, leave your jewels and gold wands in the bank and buy a revolver'.[166] In 1914, the Irish Women's Franchise League organised a 'Daffodil Fete' that included four theatrical tableaux featuring Joan of Arc performed by Markievicz.[167] In one scene (Figure 10), she liberates a female suffrage prisoner wearing full armour and carrying a sword. Although the tableau is dramatising the political enfranchisement of women, by 1914 Markievicz was well-known as an Irish revolutionary, lending the pageant a nationalist as well as a feminist message for its audience.

The Irish pageant was based on Cicely Hamilton's *A Pageant of Great Women*, a British suffrage play that 'gathered many famous names together to present a theatrical picture of female solidarity and strength that would motivate, educate and move the audience'.[168] The pageant debuted in London in

---

[163] Ibid., pp. 183–4.

[164] M. Booth, 'Jeanne d'Arc, Arab Hero: Warrior Women, Gender Confusion, and Feminine Political Authority in the Arab-Ottoman *Fin de Siècle*', in J. Cothran and Shubert (eds.), *Women Warriors*, pp. 149–77 (p. 150).

[165] C. Dubois, '"A Light in the Path to Us Women of Today": Constance Markievicz's Heroines of the Past', *Imaginaires* 23 (2021), 30–47.

[166] C. Markievicz, *Women, Ideals and the Nation* (Dublin: The Tower Press, 1909). Quoted in Dubois, 'A Light', p. 36.

[167] J. Fitzpatrick Dean, *All Dressed Up: Modern Irish Historical Pageantry* (Syracuse, NY: Syracuse University Press, 2014), p. 81.

[168] N. Paxton, *Stage Rights! The Actresses' Franchise League, Activism and Politics 1908–58* (Manchester: Manchester University Press, 2018), p. 64.

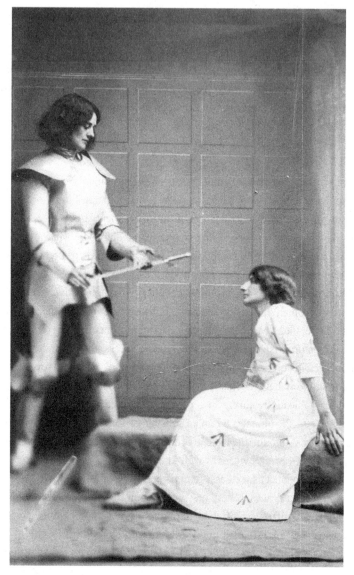

Figure 10 Photograph, 'Constance Markievicz in a pageant as Joan of Arc appearing to a woman political prisoner'. Image courtesy of the National Library of Ireland

November 1909, and then toured Britain before its final recorded performance took place in Liverpool in 1912.[169] It featured a cast of women warriors

---

[169] K. Cockin, 'Cicely Hamilton's Warriors: Dramatic Reinventions of Militancy in the British Women's Suffrage Movement', *Women's History Review* 14: 3–4 (2005), 527–42 (p. 527).

including Joan of Arc, Boadicea, Emilia Plater, Agustina de Aragón, and the Rani of Jhansi. The role of the silent group of Women Warriors in the play was to challenge the declaration by 'Prejudice', the character representing anti-suffrage arguments, that force is the last and ultimate judge: 'tis man/Who laps his body in mail, who takes the sword/The sword that must decide! Woman shrinks from it/Fears the white glint of it and cowers away'.[170] The armour-clad, sword-bearing 'Captains and Warriors' who entered the stage deny these essentialist claims about women's inability to take up combat roles. Hamilton's play thus praised armed women not only for their devotion to their causes but also for their transgression of traditional models of womanhood. However, unlike Constance Markievicz's performance of Joan of Arc that married militant feminism with armed resistance to British rule, the Warrior Women scene in Hamilton's play reinforced a colonial vision in its description of the Rani of Jhansi: 'Thou dark-eyed princess of an eastern land,/Ruler of Jhansi, captain proved in war/Though but a child in years, thou tak'st thy rank/Among thy fellows'.[171] The language here is reminiscent of British Orientalist depictions of the Rani's 'exoticism' and bravery and no mention is made of the fact that the men she was fighting were British soldiers. The Rani was played in one performance by suffragist Munci Capel, and in another by Anglo-Indian actor and suffragist Adeline Bourne.[172] Bourne was a prominent member of the Actresses' Franchise League, and after initially being 'frightened of the militants' and the potential risk to her career prospects of feminist activism, she devoted herself to the suffrage cause.[173] Bourne performed other 'Orientalist' heroines, including Cleopatra in a pageant of Shakespearean heroines for the Women Writer's Suffrage League in 1912, described as the 'climax' of the show, and Salome in Oscar Wilde's play, which a reviewer in 1911 states was indicative of a more widespread fashion for 'Easternisms in the theatre', giving a 'real atmosphere of the Arabian nights' in London.[174] Playing the Rani in Hamilton's pageant was therefore consistent with the roles in which Bourne was regularly cast during her career, although reviews did not reference her Anglo-Indian background. More importantly, however, the description of the Rani in

---

[170] C. Hamilton, *A Pageant of Great Women* (London: The Suffrage Shop, 1910), p. 39.

[171] Ibid., p. 41.

[172] Munci Capel is likely to be Mary N. U. Capel, who is listed as a donor to a suffrage society in the 1890s as 'Mrs Nelson Capel'. Women's Library Archive, *Annual Report of the National Society for Women's Suffrage*, 1897-98, GB1062NWS. Bourne's real name was Selina Manson.

[173] Paxton, *Stage Rights*, p. 114. The risk to her career prospects was a real one. In one article, the journalist cuts off her sentence 'I am a member of the Women's ...' with the retort 'We wish if you please our extensive area of office windows to remain intact'. Anon, 'Miss Adeline Bourne', *The Era*, 22 March 1913.

[174] Anon, 'A Pageant of Shakespeare's Heroines', *The Vote*, 7 February 1912; Anon, 'The Harem Skirt and Other Easternisms in the Theatre', *Graphic*, 11 March 1911.

A Pageant of Great Women reveals how Western feminists fell back on orientalist stereotypes when they used African or Indian warrior women as exemplars to support the suffrage cause, thereby eliding the racist colonial roots of the power structures against which the resistant women were fighting.

The common use of women warrior figures as mobilisation tools in global feminist and suffrage movements in the late nineteenth and early twentieth centuries is explained by a number of factors: the worldwide recognition and adaptability of Joan of Arc as a heroine, the popularity, translation and global distribution of collective biographies of 'Great Women' as a literary genre, and the desire by feminist activists for role models who could embody active female citizenship in writings, parades, pageants, and stage performances. This analysis has also shown how different aspects of the women warrior figures were foregrounded in feminist discourse, which reflected the different tactics and divergent ideological roots of the broader women's movement. Such tensions were equally apparent in responses of first-wave feminists to the deployment of female soldiers in the First World War. The outbreak of war polarised women who were active in suffrage and women's rights movements, sometimes dividing those who had worked closely together, with some rallying unproblematically to their nation's flag, and others remaining (or becoming) staunchly pacifist, defining and refining their ideological position as the war progressed.[175] These divisions can be seen in the reception of the Russian women soldiers amongst feminists. Emmeline Pankhurst, a prominent supporter of the Allied war effort, visited Russia in summer 1917 and expressed her admiration for Bochkareva's Battalion of Death, seeing in it a new basis for winning citizenship, and proclaiming to its members: 'I greet you in the name of millions and millions of women's hearts who anxiously await the results of your heroic attempts to show that women have the right and CAN participate in society in any situation and can be everywhere on the same level as men.'[176] In contrast, pacifist feminists like Emmeline's daughter Sylvia presented female combatants as part of the problem not the solution to women's oppression, perpetuating the violence that they associated with patriarchal power structures. Accordingly, in a diary entry describing Emmeline Pankhurst's visit to Russia, Sylvia described the female soldiers her mother inspected as 'ill-starred companies of women', and commented in the journal she edited, *The Female Dreadnought*, that the name the 'Battalion of Death' 'was well chosen'.[177] The same tensions were also apparent in the United States. Journalist Bessy Beatty, one of several

---

[175] A. S. Fell and I. Sharp, 'Introduction', in A. S. Fell and I. Sharp (eds.), *The Women's Movement in Wartime: International Perspectives* (Basingstoke: Palgrave, 2007), pp. 1–17.

[176] Quoted in Stoff, *They Fought for the Motherland*, p. 199.

[177] Ibid., p. 200; Anon, 'Questions of the Day', *The Woman's Dreadnought*, 30 June 1917.

female American journalists who reported on Russia in 1917, saw in the women soldiers a vision of a new society: 'Not the isolated individual woman who has buckled on a sword and shouldered a gun through the pages of history, but the woman soldier banded and fighting *on masse* – gun companies of her, battalions of her, whole regiments of her'.[178] On the other side of the argument, Louise Bryant, a socialist feminist who published another eye-witness account entitled *Six Red Months in Russia*, attacked them as class traitors in their role of shaming peasant men into enlisting.[179] Russian women soldiers were also regularly attacked by anti-suffragists who questioned their 'mannish' appearance and morality, and saw in them a doomed future for mankind. Once again, the familiar tropes of sexual immorality, lesbianism, and anti-feminine behaviours used to demonise armed women were never far from the surface in debates about armed women during this period.

4 Women Warriors, Demobilisation, and Post-War Memory Cultures

The previous section has shown that the popularity of the woman warrior archetype as a model of brave devotion to nation meant it could be an effective mobilisation strategy when global women's rights movements were attempting to broaden their appeal and convert new followers to their cause. However, this was more evident in the case of hero-martyrs than with living female combatants like the Russian First World War women soldiers, who received a more mixed reception among feminists. This relates to the broader point that the majority of women warriors whose images and stories were instrumentalised by a range of state and non-state actors to mobilise populations in times of war, revolution, or in resistance movements had no say about the ways in which they were (mis)represented. If they had died in battle, like the Rani of Jhansi, then their cultural afterlives were entirely in the hands of others. As this Element has demonstrated, after their death women warriors could be used as figureheads for groups with opposing aims and ideologies. However, some of the women warriors whose stories I have evoked survived the wars in which they fought, and were able to take a more active role in shaping their reputations and representations. This could involve petitioning states for military pensions or other forms of financial compensation, writing autobiographies, giving talks and performances about their military action, or posing for photographs and making public appearances wearing uniforms, medals, and/or displaying arms. In doing so, they were making a claim for the value of their war service, and

---

[178] B. Beatty, *The Red Heart of Russia* (New York: The Century Company, 1918), p. 91.
[179] L. Bryant, *Six Red Months in Russia* (New York: George H. Doran, 1918).

demanding both respect and recognition from their peacetime audiences. In this section, I analyse how women warriors attempted to present themselves as veterans, and the extent to which their claims to veteran status were accepted or rejected by post-conflict societies.

Women who took up combat roles had different motivations for wishing to preserve their wartime identities in peacetime. Some were motivated by economic hardship as well as a desire for acclaim and recognition by the state, by other veterans, and/or by broader publics. One route to the promotion of their stories was by publishing war memoirs. This was the case with both Maria Bochkareva and Lyudmila Pavlichenko. There was a ready market for the autobiographies of women soldiers, which drew on longer literary traditions as well as benefiting from publishing booms in 'war books' that followed both world wars. Bochkareva was illiterate and published her 1919 memoir, *Yashka: My Life as Peasant, Officer and Exile*, with the help of an émigré journalist living in the United States, Isaac Don Levine, who claimed in his preface that Bochkareva 'recited to me in Russian the story of her life, and I recorded it in English in longhand'.[180] Her narrative was therefore mediated, and largely conforms to a tsarist war narrative of patriotic bravery in defence of the sacred homeland, attacking Bolshevism as a 'nightmare of revolution and terror'.[181] Yet it equally emphasises her resistance to patriarchal oppression as she details the unequal treatment she had received as a female worker and soldier, and the abuse she had suffered at the hands of violent and drunken men. She overtly challenges other media accounts of her life and motivations that had constructed her as a devoted wife who enlisted to avenge her husband, a familiar trope in cultural representations of women warriors. Her rejection of gender norms in the narrative is also evident in her replacement of the socially acceptable identity of a 'veiled ... Englishwoman returning home' that she was forced to take on when fleeing Russia for the United States with that of celebrated representative of the 'Russian peasant-soldier' as soon as she arrived.[182] Bochkareva's purpose in publishing her life story was not only to make a claim for her identity as a soldier, but equally to encourage Allied intervention into the Russian Civil War on the side of the Whites. Her existing connections with influential members of the women's movement and Russian émigré circles, as well as her story-telling ability and experience with presenting herself in public as a woman warrior, led her to meet President Woodrow Wilson and to exert a degree of political influence.[183] However, published in English in the

---

[180] I. D. Levine, 'Introduction', in Botchkareva, *Yashka*, p. 1.   [181] Ibid., p. 244.
[182] Ibid., p. 259.   [183] F. J. Harriman, *From Pinafores to Politics* (New York: Henry Holt, 1923).

United States, her memoirs did not influence public opinion in Russia, nor did they protect her from her arrest and execution by the Bolsheviks after her return.

In contrast, Lyudmila Pavlichenko's memoirs, *Lady Death: The Memoirs of Stalin's Sniper*, were first published in Russian before being translated into English, and to some extent reflected her success in carving out a post-war identity as a heroic Soviet war veteran. Highly decorated during the war, Pavlichenko finished her training as a historian after 1945 and joined the Research Institute of the Soviet Navy, leaving in 1953 with the rank of Major (and accompanying Officer's pension) before becoming active in the Soviet Committee of War Veterans.[184] Despite the accolades and her acceptance as a war hero by post-war Soviet society, however, she stated in her memoirs that she increasingly suffered from shellshock, and died from alcoholism aged fifty-eight in 1974. The published version of her life story was based on manuscript fragments that were pieced together by her daughter-in-law. Pavlichenko's auto-biography is patriotic in tone, but her narrative voice is very different from that of Bochkareva. The narrator paints the portrait not only of an exceptional and devoted soldier but also of a reliable witness to war, offering an informed analysis of high command decisions as well as a personal account of her experiences as a combatant. In her account of fighting a 'sacred war . . . wreak[ing] vengeance on a treacherous enemy', Pavlichenko presents herself as a successful cog in a well-oiled machine, without making frequent references to her gender or to patriarchal resistance to her combat role.[185] Despite their adherence to mainstream Soviet war narratives, however, Pavlichenko's memoirs also tell a tale of psychological breakdown and lament the damage to minds and bodies wrought by war, an interpretation that was perhaps more possible in the 1960s than it had been in earlier decades. Equally, other evidence reveals that Pavlichenko, one of the most securely established Soviet war heroines, still faced accusations of sexual immorality and false heroism. Amandine Regamey quotes from a letter Pavlichenko wrote in 1946 that outlined the criticism she was facing and demanded that Mikhailov, president of the Komsomol Central Committee, took action to protect her reputation. As Regamey argues, Pavlichenko's hero status did not fully protect her from the usual criticisms levied at women warriors, but unlike other female combatants facing similar attacks 'as a Hero she enjoyed resources and connections that enabled her to challenge the accusation'.[186]

---

[184] M. Pegler, 'Forward', in L. Pavlichenko (ed.), *Lady Death: The Memoirs of Stalin's Sniper* (Barnsley: Greenhill Books, 2018), p. xiii.

[185] Ibid., p. 51.

[186] A. Regamey, 'Soviet Women Snipers: Experiences of Fire', paper presented at 'Annihilation and Resilience: The Soviet War and PostWar, 1939–1968', Berlin, 29–30 January 2015. www.academia.edu/download/36492911/Soviet_women_snipers_experiences_of_fire.pdf.

Another strategy for women warriors who attempted to construct a post-conflict role as a veteran was to petition for state recognition and/or financial compensation for their war service. This was the case for Nene Hatun, veteran of the Ottoman-Russian War of 1877–8, Serbian soldier Milunka Savić, who fought in the First World War, and Mexican revolutionary Amelio Robles. In 1943, and in her eighties, Hatun, along with Name Hamim, another woman who had participated in the defence of the Aziziye Bastion, petitioned the Turkish authorities for support and recognition, describing their armed participation in the defence of Turkey as a 'miracle of world history', and emphasising their dire financial straits, claiming that the municipal authorities in Erzurum had cut their daily rations leaving them destitute.[187] However, this letter was ignored and Hatun was only awarded a monthly state pension after Turkey became a member of NATO in 1952, which brought about her 're-discovery' as a war heroine by journalists, and led to her being singled out by US General Matthew Bunker Ridgway, NATO Supreme Commander of the Allied Forces. The new political context, and particularly the prominence of anti-Soviet discourse, created a need for national heroes like Hatun who had fought the Russians and who could be presented as 'Mothers of the Nation'. As an elderly veteran of a nineteenth-century war, Hatun also became a figure of international interest in the 1950s press. A 1952 British newspaper article by journalist Henry Thody, for example, compared Hatun to the Home Guard in the Second World War:

> The real value of the Turk, old or new, is [a] terrible toughness. . . . I went down a narrow street to visit 97-year-old Nene Hatun, sole survivor of the famous Home Guard battle of 1877. . . . Nene slowly told me of the battle. . . . [My husband] told me to stay at home with the baby, but how could I stay at home on such a day? . . . "Did you kill any Russians?" I asked the old lady. She looked at me scornfully. "We all killed Russians that day".[188]

Thody presented her as a brave but exotically 'savage' woman warrior, drawing on stereotypes reminiscent of the descriptions of Albanian warrior Tringë Smajli Martini Juncaj that appeared in the Western press in 1911. But he also viewed her as an anachronism in modern Turkey, echoing the broader theme of the article that NATO membership was modernising a 'primitive' nation. On 30 August 1952, the thirtieth anniversary of Turkish victory in the Greco-Turkish war, Hatun was guest of honour at the inauguration of a new statue commemorating 1877. A Turkish newspaper described her as a 'living monument' of the birth of the Turkish state, fulfilling the desire she had expressed in

---

[187] Turkish Presidency State Archives of the Republic of Turkey, 030.10 (General Directorate for Documentation), 120.858.17, August 26, 1943, 1. Cited in Emen-Gokatalay, 'Popularising and Promoting Nene Hatun', p. 52.

[188] H. Thody, 'Most Frightening Home Guard in the World', *Western Mail*, 16 September 1952.

her petition ten years earlier to be recognised for her patriotic service.[189] Hatun died in 1955, and her hero myth continued to grow after her death. For the centenary commemoration of the Ottoman-Russian War in 1977, for example, her tomb formed the central piece of a newly renovated monument at Aziziye, and in more recent decades she has become firmly established as a national heroine.

Alongside Antonia Javornik (Natalia Bjelajac), Sofia Jovanović, Živana Terzić, and British woman Flora Sandes, Milunka Savić fought for the Serbian army in the First World War.[190] Savić had already participated in the Balkan Wars, dressed as a man, and was initially turned down when offering her services to the army as a volunteer. She was eventually accepted into the Rudnički volunteer unit, served in the Assault Bomb section, and was promoted and awarded the Gold Order of Mercy. Her story and photograph were widely circulated as a model of female patriotic service and Allied cooperation under fire, especially in France, where she was hospitalised in 1916.[191] For one propaganda postcard, for example, she was photographed posing alongside the French and Serbian flags (Figure 11). In 1917 she was awarded the French Legion of Honour, and after the war was offered a French pension that she turned down. In interwar Belgrade, she struggled financially as a single mother, and her story was largely forgotten or ignored. This is explained to some extent by post-war memory culture for Serbs who had fought in the First World War. In the 1920s, after the formation of the Kingdom of Serbs, Croats, and Slovenes, war memory was complicated by the fact that the Kingdom included war dead and veterans from both sides of the conflict. An attempt was made to produce a more inclusive all-Yugoslav line of commemoration in the pan-Yugoslav monument at Avala, but more often it was Serbian heroism that was emphasised in evocations of the war, and this proved more divisive than unifying.[192] As Jason Hansen argues, war memorials did not acknowledge Croat, Slovene, or Bosnian veterans' memories. They equally left no room for remembering women's contributions.[193] It was within this broader context that Savić actively

---

[189] Anon, 'Aziziye Abidesi Törenle Açilki' ('Opening Ceremony of Aziziye Monument'), *Cumhuriyet*, 3 September 1952, quoted in B. Bilmez, 'Hero Women in the Turkish Popular Memory of the Russo-Ottoman War (1877–1878): Presentation of Nene Hatun as an Eternal Heroine in the Popular Media', *Balkanistic Forum* 3 (2016), 77–108 (p. 84).

[190] B. Mladenović, 'Women's Mobilization for War (South East Europe)', *1914-1918-online. International Encyclopedia of the First World War*, https://doi.org/10.15463/ie1418.10167.

[191] F. Solar, 'Une Héroïne Serbe', *Le Petit Marseillais*, 7 May 1916.

[192] J. P. Newman, *Yugoslavia in the Shadow of War: Veterans and the Limit of State Building* (Cambridge: Cambridge University Press, 2015).

[193] J. Hansen, 'The Forgotten Front? Serbian Memory and the First World War', in R. B. McCormick, A. Hernandez-Laroche and C. G. Canino (eds.), *An International Rediscovery of World War 1: Distant Fronts* (London: Routledge, 2020), pp. 35–53.

CAMPAGNE D'ORIENT 1914-15-1916

L'HÉROINE SERBE
MILOUNKA STAVITZ
19 ans, 3 années de Guerre, 3 blessures graves

Figure 11 'L'Héroïne Serbe Milounka Stavitz (sic)' (Serbian Heroine Milunka
Savić), French First World War postcard

attempted to sustain her identity as a heroic war veteran. For example, a 1922
newspaper article in the *Chicago Tribune* publicised her request to be 'adopted'
by an American family to escape her poverty:

> Today the war is over. My father is dead. My mother has married again. All
> my friends were killed in the war. I work here in the hospital in Belgrade
> but ... I am poor. In the war, life was always brave and happy. Today, it is

always sad – always the struggle for food, for clothes, for life. .... I wish
I could live in the old days, for to live now is to be dead.[194]

In another telling comment in the article, she emphasised that she was not
looking for marriage proposals, but insisted on her identity as a veteran: 'I don't
want to marry a foolish man who writes letters to the pictures of girls in
newspapers. I have been a soldier. I understand those things about foolish
men'. Her attempt to carve out a new life as a veteran-heroine in the United
States failed, although she did travel to France in 1931 where she was honoured
by French veteran associations at a banquet as a 'glorious Serbian combatant',
and congratulated by the French president as a representative of the ongoing
'friendship between France and Yugoslavia'.[195] But she remained relatively
unknown in Belgrade, working as a postal worker and then as a cleaner. She
adopted three daughters in addition to her own, the result of a short unsuccessful
marriage, and then paid for more children from her village to be educated in
Belgrade. In the Second World War, she hid and cared for members of the anti-
fascist resistance movement in her house.[196] In 1945 she was awarded a state
pension, and given an apartment. Her working-class credentials made her
a good fit for the communists' anti-capitalist take on the memory of the First
World War. However, it was only in the decades following her death in 1973,
and especially in the years following the collapse of Yugoslavia, that she was
more successfully rebranded as a Serbian hero with wider symbolic resonances.
On 10 November 2013, Savić was reburied in Belgrade, and was compared by
the president to the nation of Serbia itself: 'Milunka Savić so resembles the
country. Courageous when needed, invincible and upright, ready to help every-
one, but again pushed aside when others think that she might get in the way,
being so great and strong'.[197]

Hatun's and Savić's transformations into 'Mothers of the Nation' after their
deaths, effectively mainstreaming the more radical aspects of their identity as
women demanding state recompense for military service, is reminiscent of the
case of Amelio Robles, who fought in the 1910 Mexican Revolution and then
joined the Mexican Army in the early 1920s. Robles participated as a woman
before living as a transgender man for the rest of his life. As a Zaptista guerrilla,
Robles adopted the clothing, pose, and behaviours of a male fighter, and was

---

[194] O. Swift, 'People's Chance to Adopt Serb Modern Joan', *Chicago Tribune*, 4 April 1922.
[195] Anon, 'M. Charpentier de Ribes préside le banquet des Poilus d'Orient', *Le Matin*, 7 June 1931;
Anon, 'Chez M. Doumergue', *Le Progrès de la Côte d'Or*, 7 June 1931.
[196] Blog, 'La Serbie s'invite: entretien avec Sladana Zarić', 20 January 2015, http://femmesenuni
forme.blogspot.com/2015/01/la-serbie-sinvite-interview-de-slaana.html.
[197] Quoted in Hansen, 'The Forgotten Front', p. 46.

accepted as a man until his death aged ninety-four.[198] In the decades following the Revolution, Robles did not receive a military pension, but he continued to be politically active, fighting alongside other Zapatista guerrillas to keep collective land ownership, and for agrarian reforms. In his lifetime, his identity as a male veteran was accepted: a local school was named after him in 1966, and in 1974 he was recognised by the Ministry of National Defence as an official veteran of the Revolution, partly because some of the guerrillas he had fought alongside had influential political and military roles.[199] His acceptance by the authorities as a male veteran was important for his social status, as the pension law assumed that recipients were male heads of household.[200] After his death in 1984, however, Robles was re-feminised and re-imagined as a female revolutionary. In 1989, for example, a community museum was established that celebrated Robles as a woman warrior, an initiative that was backed by family members and the Mexican Ministry for Women. In a move reminiscent of the 're-discovery' of some African women warriors, Robles became a useful symbol of female empowerment for a government keen to promote increased social and economic participation for women, but this recognition also mis-gendered him. It was only in the twenty-first century that Robles has been re-presented as a transgender man, celebrated by LGBTQ activists.[201]

The actions and writings of Nene Hatun, Milunka Savić, and Amelio Robles reveal that they were proud of their identities as war veterans, and proactively sought political influence, wider recognition, and financial compensation for their military service. However, it was only in old age, and to an even greater extent after their deaths, that they gained full status as national heroes. This is explained by the evolving political contexts in Turkey, Yugoslavia/Serbia, and Mexico. Their pleas for financial support and recognition alongside their fellow veterans in peacetime often went unheeded, but they once again proved useful figureheads when their nations were seeking inspirational role models who could embody what was understood as a gender-appropriate version of national identity. Another interesting aspect of their cases is the extent to which their fame and status were enhanced by international political and media interest in their stories. Hetan proved a useful symbol for the Supreme Commander of NATO in his diplomatic mission, Savić was used by French propagandists and

---

[198] G. Cano, 'Gender and Transgender in the Mexican Revolution: The Shifting Memory of Amelio Robles', in B. Cothran, J. Judge, and A. Shubert (eds.), *Women Warriors*, pp. 179–95.
[199] Ibid., p. 184.
[200] T. Rath, *Myths of Demilitarization in Postrevolutionary Mexico 1920–1960* (Chapel Hill, NC: University of North Carolina Press, 2013), p. 149.
[201] See for example Amelio Robles Ávila | Legacy Project Chicago, https://legacyprojectchicago .org/person/amelio-robles-avila.

politicians as a symbol of the Franco-Serbian political alliance during and after the First World War, and Robles' photograph posing in military uniform is now widely circulated within and beyond North America as an example of an LGBTQ hero.

However, of the thousands of women who participated in resistance and revolutionary movements in combatant roles, the majority were unsuccessful in their attempts to gain widespread recognition as veterans, to claim pensions or other forms of financial compensation, or to pursue continuing political identities as resistant women when their side was defeated. In the 1918 Finnish Civil War, many of the female combatants who had fought for the Reds were raped or killed after the victory of the Whites. Over 5,000 Red women were charged with treason, and as part of these charges their sexual morality was frequently questioned alongside their status as revolutionaries. The 14 per cent who were convicted had to temporarily forfeit their civil rights.[202] In the aftermath of the Spanish Civil War (1936–9), the *milicianas* who had fought for the Republican cause were similarly subject to humiliation and economic and social repression, and many were raped and imprisoned. Gina Herrmann's evidence from oral history interviews suggests that amongst survivors it was largely men who continued to participate in anti-fascist or anti-Franco resistance activities, while the women 'either dropped out entirely or worked in a limited capacity', although she includes the example of a former *miliciana* who campaigned with her husband for the Spanish government to pay reparations to Republican combatants wounded in the war.[203] In Ireland, around 18,000 men and women were awarded military pensions on the basis of the service they had given in various revolutionary organisations (or for the Irish Army) between 1916 and 1923.[204] Following the 1924 Military Service Pensions Act, there were attempts to exclude women on the basis of their gender, including women who had been wounded, from being awarded military pensions. Margaret Skinnider, for example, who was shot and badly wounded in the Easter Rising, had her application refused on the basis that the Act was 'only applicable to soldiers as generally understood in the masculine sense'.[205] As Marie Coleman argues, however, Skinnider's anti-Treaty stance is also likely to have played a role in the decision not to award the pension. In 1932 and 1949,

---

[202] T. Lintunen, 'Women at War', in T. Tepora and A. Roselius (eds.), *The Finnish Civil War 1918* (Leiden: Brill, 2014), pp. 201–29 (p. 226).

[203] G. Herrmann, 'Voices of the Vanquished: Leftist Women and the Spanish Civil War', *Journal of Spanish Cultural Studies* 4:1 (2013), 11–29, p. 12.

[204] M. Coleman, 'Compensating Irish Female Revolutionaries, 1916–1923', *Women's History Review* 26:6 (2017), 915–34 (p. 916).

[205] Treasury Solicitor to Army Finance Officer, 18 March 1925, MSPC, W1P724: Margaret Skinnider. Quoted in Ibid., p. 921.

further Pensions Acts were passed that cast the net much wider in terms of who was included.[206] Crucially, membership of the Republican women's paramilitary organisation Cumann na mBan made women eligible for a military pension, which enabled hundreds of women, including Skinnider, to successfully apply for military pensions, mostly for non-combatant service. As was the case with Hetan and Savić, economic hardship was one motivation for the pension applications, but appeals in the Irish pension files also reveal a desire on the part of applicants for equal recognition with men in the movements they participated in. Furthermore, gender remained a key factor in how Irish women's war service was understood and compensated: as Coleman concludes, in post-1923 Ireland 'the female veteran was very much the poor relation among the old comrades of the Irish revolution'.[207]

These examples reveal that demobilisation offered relatively few routes for women to take an active role in their cultural constructions and post-conflict reputations as warriors or war heroines. While a handful received awards, recognition, and/or financial compensation from the state, others faced humiliation, mistreatment, or abuse. There was also less space on the public stage for women warriors once their primary function of mobilisation was no longer needed. Post-conflict societies tended rather to focus on the politics of reconstruction or reconciliation, and as a consequence the emphasis was on women's traditional roles as wives, carers, and producers of future citizen-soldiers. This explains why gender non-conforming warriors such as Amelio Robles were sometimes 're-feminised' after their deaths to fit in with prevailing social and gender norms. However, the recent re-discovery of Robles as a role model for the global trans rights movement demonstrates how the uses of the woman warrior archetype have continued to evolve into the twenty-first century.

I began this Element with a discussion of *Wonder Woman* to demonstrate the persistence of age-old stereotypes of the woman warrior, arguing that the film illustrates the importance of palimpsestic memory as a model to understand the cultural representation of armed women in modern warfare. However, a key aspect of palimpsests is their continual evolution as further layers are added. In the twenty-first century, the women warriors who were active in conflicts between the 1850s and 1945 have continued to be re-imagined and re-evoked to suit new political contexts and fresh agendas. Take, for example, the warrior women who were known in the West as the 'Dahomey Amazons', an all-female army from the Kingdom of Dahomey (within present-day Republic of Benin). At the time of the Franco-Dahomey Wars in the 1890s, these African women

---

[206] M. Coleman, 'Military Service Pensions for Veterans of the Irish Revolution', *War in History* 20:2 (2013), 201–21.

[207] Coleman, 'Compensating Irish Female Revolutionaries', p. 930.

warriors had been regularly mythologised as 'Amazons' in European journalism and travel writing. Richard Burton's 1864 ethnographic account, *Mission to Gelele, King of Dahomé* produced illustrations of the armed women who fought for their Kingdom that drew on stereotypical nineteenth-century representations of the Amazons.[208] Orientalist representations of African warriors not only reproduced racist understandings of 'barbaric' African societies but also bore witness to 'a tension between the Amazon's presumed need for imperial civilization and her ability to thwart it through an assertion of her own alluring authority'.[209] The 'Dahomey Amazons' were presented as fascinating objects of desire for the consumption of Western readers and spectators. This related to the broader cultural phenomenon of 'Human Zoos': in the late nineteenth century, dehumanising exhibitions of exotic and 'primitive' populations were a form of mass entertainment. This included performances such as John Wood's dance troupe, supposedly composed of 'Dahomean Amazons', that toured Europe. Dahomean women were also exhibited at Exhibitions and World Fairs, such as the World Exhibition in Paris in 1877, and the Columbian Exposition in Chicago in 1893, which both featured a 'Dahomey village'.[210] These representations of African women warriors served to prop up White European identities, conveying 'a sense of racial Otherness, embodied as black and exteriorized in "Africa," essential to generating a shared affect of belonging to Europeanness-as-whiteness'.[211] In the twenty-first century, however, these West African women warriors have taken on a new resonance in novels, films and other cultural productions influenced by decolonial and Afrofuturist movements seeking to celebrate pre-colonial models of Black African identity. The 2018 Marvel film *Black Panther* is an example of this cultural trend.[212] The film's characters Dora Milaje and Nakia demand respect for their military prowess, and exercise political agency, making up half of the governing body of the fictional Kingdom of Wakanda.[213] Such representations expose and subvert the exoticised and sexualised cultural representations of 'Dahomey Amazons' in nineteenth-century colonial travel writing. These new

---

[208] M. E. Adams, 'The Amazon Warrior Woman and de/construction of Gendered Imperial Authority in Nineteenth-Century Colonial Literature', *Nineteenth Century Gender Studies* 6:1 (2010), www.ncgsjournal.com/issue61/adams.html.

[209] Ibid.

[210] Larsen, 'Wives and Warriors', p. 230; I. Novikova, 'Imagining Africa and Blackness in the Russian Empire: From Extra-textual *arapka* and Distant Cannibals to Dahomey Amazon Shows live in Moscow and Riga', *Social Identities* 19:5 (2013), 571–91, https://doi.org/10.1080/13504630.2013.810122.

[211] Novikova, 'Imagining Africa', p. 586.   [212] *Black Panther* (2018), dir. R. Coogler.

[213] E. Abena Osei, 'Wakanda Africa do you see? Reading Black Panther as a decolonial film through the lens of the Sankofa theory', *Critical Studies in Media Communication* 37:4 (2020), 378–90, https://doi.org/10.1080/15295036.2020.1820538.

visions of African women warriors demonstrate not only the continued importance of the woman warrior as a cultural archetype, but also the extent to which this archetype can be understood as an example of 'travelling memory', taking on new meanings and performing different functions as it embodies evolving understandings of women's relationship to war and combat.

Bibliography

Primary Sources

Archival Sources

Imperial War Museum (IWM)
'Joan of Arc Saved France', Poster, 1918, Art.IWM PST10297.

Bibliothèque Nationale Française (BNF)
Dupré, M., 'Yanitza, cantate pour 3 voix et orchestre', 1912, MS autogr., MS17634.
Paray, P., 'Yanitza, cantate avec orchestre', 1911, MS autogr., MS6457.

Museum of London
H. Serjeant, Postcard with a photograph of a statue of Joan of Arc, 1913, 50.82/923 c.

National Film and Sound Archive of Australia
'The Joan of Arc of Loos: Original Release', 1916, 572222.

National Archives and Records Administration, College Park, Maryland
Photograph, Raymonde Breton visits her sister Louise in the Signal Corps barracks at Neufchateau, 1918, 111-SC-50699.

National Library of Ireland
H. R. McMahon, Photograph, Constance Markievicz in a pageant as Joan of Arc appearing to a woman political prisoner, 1914, NPA POLF201.

Women's Library Archives
Annual Report of the National Society for Women's Suffrage, 1897–98, GB1062NWS.

Military Service Pensions Collection, Ireland (MSPC)
Treasury Solicitor to Army Finance Officer, 18 March 1925, W1P724: Margaret Skinnider.

Public Records Office of Northern Ireland (PRONI)
Edith Londonderry, 'The Women's Legion, 1914', 1944, D3099/14/1.

South Asian American Digital Archive (SAADA)
'Rani Lakshmi Bai: Heroine of the War of Independence of 1857', *The United States of India*, May 1926, Gadar Party Collection, www.saada.org/item/201 11129-508.

Turkish Presidency State Archives of the Republic of Turkey
Letter from Nene Hatun, 030.10 (General Directorate for Documentation),
120.858.17, 26 August 1943, 1.

Films
Black Panther, dir. R. Coogler, 2018.
Fräulein Doktor, dir. A. Lattuada, 1969.
Fräulein Feldgrau, dir. C. Wilhelm, 1915.
Fräulein Leutnant, dir. C. Wilhelm, 1914.
The Joan of Arc of Loos, dir. G. Willoughby, 1916.
Joan the Woman, dir. C.B. De Mille, 1916.
Mademoiselle Docteur, dir. G.W. Pabst, 1937.
'Women's Volunteer Reserve Marching', Pathé films, 1917.
Wonder Woman, dir. P. Jenkins, 2017.

Newspaper and Magazine Articles

Anon, 'M. Charpentier de Ribes préside le banquet des Poilus d'Orient'
(M. Charpentier de Ribes presides over the banquet for French veterans
who served in the East) *Le Matin*, 7 June 1931.
Anon, 'Chez M. Doumergue' (With M. Doumergue) *Le Progrès de la Côte
d'Or*, 7 June 1931.
Anon, 'Miss Adeline Bourne', *The Era*, 22 March 1913.
Anon, 'Aziziye Abidesi Törenle Açilki' ('Opening Ceremony of Aziziye
Monument'), *Cumhuriyet*, 3 September 1952.
Anon, 'English Women Aid in Getting Recruits', *New York Times*, 26 June
1915.
Anon, 'Albanian Joan of Arc: Handsome Heroine Takes Father's Place and
Vanquishes Turks', *New York Times*, 21 May 1911.
Anon, 'The Harem Skirt and Other Easternisms in the Theatre', *Graphic*,
11 March 1911.
Anon, 'Impressive Protest at the Opera', *The Suffragette*, 19 December 1913.
Anon, 'I Will Lead You', *Pall Mall Gazette*, 5 May 1911.
Anon, 'Les femmes à l'armée' (Women in the army), *Excelsior*, 28 April 1915.
Anon, 'Jeannes d'Arc' (Joans of Arc), *La Jeunesse Illustrée*, 17 December
1911.
Anon, 'Japan's Joan of Arc', *The World's News* (Sydney), 22 November 1933.
Anon, 'La vie des héroïnes Russes à la caserne' (Life of Russian heroines in the
barracks), *Le Miroir*, 19 August 1917.
Anon, 'Lettre de Serbie' (Letter from Serbia), *Le Soir*, 25 August 1876.
Anon, 'The New Russia', *Reading Observer*, 1 September 1917.

Anon, 'Joan of Arc of Loos', *Sydney Evening News*, 2 May 1916.

Anon, 'The New Russia', *Reading Observer*, 1 September 1917.

Anon, 'A Pageant of Shakespeare's Heroines', *The Vote*, 7 February 1912.

Anon, 'Questions of the Day', *The Woman's Dreadnought*, 30 June 1917.

Anon, 'A West African Joan of Arc', *Western Evening Herald*, 11 January 1896.

Anon, 'Women are Not Killers – ATS Chief', *Courier and Advertiser*, 1 October 1942.

Anon, 'Pavlichenko's Tribute to City', *Liverpool Evening Express*, 24 November 1942.

Anon, 'Suffragettes at the Opera', *Western Gazette*, 19 December 1913.

Anon, 'Forty Eight Women Against Hitler', *Daily News*, 7 November 1942.

Denson, G. R., 'The Wonder Woman "No Man's Land" Scene is Rooted in History, Myth and Art', *HuffPost*, 5 August 2017.

Killian, K. D., 'How Wonder Woman is and isn't a Feminist Superheroine Movie', *Psychology Today*, 19 June 2018.

Laut, E., 'Les Emules de Jeanne d'Arc' (The emulators of Joan of Arc), *Le Petit Journal Supplément*, 28 May 1911.

Solar, F., 'Une Héroïne Serbe' (A Serbian heroine), *Le Petit Marseillais*, 7 May 1916.

Swift, O., 'People's Chance to Adopt Serb Modern Joan', *Chicago Tribune*, 4 April 1922.

Thody, H., 'Most Frightening Home Guard in the World', *Western Mail*, 16 September 1952.

Printed Primary Sources

Anand, M., *Across the Black Waters* (New Dehli: Orient Paperbacks, 2008).

Anon, *Jai-Hind: The Diary of a Rebel Daughter of India with the Rani of Jhansi Regiment* (Bombay: Janmabhoomi Prakashan Mandir, 1945).

Anon, *Des deutschen Volkes Kriegstagebuch* (Leipzig: Philipp Reclam, 1915).

Beatty, B., *The Red Heart of Russia* (New York: The Century, 1918).

Botchkareva, M. and Levine, D.L., *Yashka: My Life as Peasant, Officer and Exile* (New York: Frederick A. Stokes, 1919).

Bryant, L., *Six Red Months in Russia* (New York: George H. Doran, 1918).

Cox, P., *The Rani of Jhansi: A Historical Play in Four Acts* (London: Heinemann, 1933).

Durham, E. M., *High Albania* (London: Edward Arnold, 1909).

Hamilton Armitage, C. and Forbes Montanaro, A., *The Ashante Campaign of 1900* (London: Sands, 1901).

Hamilton, C., *A Pageant of Great Women* (London: The Suffrage Shop, 1910).

Harriman, F. J., *From Pinafores to Politics* (New York: Henry Holt, 1923).

Judson, W. V., *Russia in War and Revolution: General William V. Judson's Accounts from Petrograd, 1917–18* (Kent, OH: Kent State University Press, 1998).

Lawrence, D., *Sapper Dorothy Lawrence: The Only English Woman Soldier, late Royal Engineers, 51st Division, 179th Tunnelling Company, BEF* (London: John Lane, 1919).

Markievicz, C., *Women, Ideals and the Nation* (Dublin: The Tower Press, 1909).

Nehru, J., *Glimpses of World History* (Bombay: Asia Publishing House, 1967).

Pavlichenko, L., *Lady Death: The Memoirs of Stalin's Sniper* (Barnsley: Greenhill Books, 2018).

Poole, E., *Russian Impressions* (New York: Macmillan, 1918).

Sergeyev-Tsensky, S., *Brusilov's Breakthrough* (London: Hutchinson, 1945).

White, M., *Lachmi Bai: The Jeanne d'Arc of India* (New York: J.F. Taylor, 1901).

Secondary Sources

Abena Osei, E., 'Wakanda Africa Do You See? Reading Black Panther as a Decolonial Film through the Lens of the Sankofa Theory', *Critical Studies in Media Communication* 37:4 (2020), 378–90, https://doi.org/10.1080/15295036.2020.1820538.

Alpern, S. B., *Amazons of Black Sparta: The Women Warriors of Dahomey* (New York: New York University Press, 1998).

Aston, E., 'Male Impersonators in the Music-Hall: The Case of Vesta Tilley', *New Theatre Quarterly* 4:15 (1988), 247–57.

Baker, C., 'A Different Kind of Power: Identification, Stardom and Embodiments of the Military in Wonder Woman', *Critical Studies on Security* 6:3 (2018), 359–65.

Becker, A. and Audoin-Rouzeau, S., *1914–1918: Understanding the Great War* (London: Profile Books, 2002).

Bilmez, B., 'Hero Women in the Turkish Popular Memory of the Russo-Ottoman War (1877–1878): Presentation of Nene Hatun as an Eternal Heroine in the Popular Media', *Balkanistic Forum* 3 (2016), 77–108.

Birnbaum, P., *Manchu Princess, Japanese Spy: The Story of Yoshiko Kawashima, the Cross-Dressing Spy who Commanded Her Own Army* (New York: Columbia University Press, 2017).

Blobaum, R. and Blobaum, D., 'A Different Kind of Home Front: War, Gender and Propaganda in Warsaw, 1914-1918', in T. Paddock (ed.), *World War 1 and Propaganda* (Leiden: Brill, 2014), pp. 249–72.

Boahen, A. A., *Yaa Asantewaa and the Asante-British War of 1900–1* (Accra: Sub-Saharan Publishers, 2003).

Booth, A., *How to Make it as a Woman: Collective Biographical History from Victoria to the Present* (Chicago: University of Chicago Press, 2004).

Booth, M., 'The Egyptian Lives of Jeanne d'Arc', in L. Abu-Lughod (ed.), *Remaking Women: Feminism and Modernity in the Middle East* (Princeton, NJ: Princeton University Press, 1998), pp. 171–214.

Booth, M., 'Jeanne d'Arc, Arab Hero: Warrior Women, Gender Confusion, and Feminine Political Authority in the Arab-Ottoman *Fin de Siècle*', in B. Cothran, J. Judge, and A. Shubert (eds.), *Women Warriors and National Heroes* (London: Bloomsbury, 2020), pp. 149–77.

Borda, J. L., 'The Woman Suffrage Parades of 1910–1913: Possibilities and Limitations of an Early Feminist Rhetorical Strategy', *Western Journal of Communication* 66:1 (2002), 25–52, https://doi.org/10.1080/1057031020 9374724.

Boxwell, D.A., 'The Follies of War: Cross-Dressing and Popular Theatre on the British Front', *Modernisms/Modernity* 9:1 (2002), 1–20.

Brandt, B., 'Germania in Armor: Female Representation of an Endangered German Nation', in S. Colvin and H. Watanabe-O'Kelly (eds.), *Women and Death 2: Warlike Women in the German Literary and Cultural Imagination Since 1500* (Rochester, NY: Camden House, 2000), pp. 86–126.

Campbell, D., 'Women in Combat: The World War II Experience in the United States, Great Britain, Germany and the Soviet Union', *Journal of Military History* 57:2 (1993), 301–23.

Cano, G., 'Gender and Transgender in the Mexican Revolution: The Shifting Memory of Amelio Robles', in B. Cothran, J. Judge, and A. Shubert. (eds.), *Women Warriors and National Heroes* (London: Bloomsbury, 2020), pp. 179–95.

Carrier, N. and Nyamweru, C., 'Reinventing Africa's National Heroes: The Case of Mkatilili, a Kenyan Popular Heroine', *African Affairs* 115: 461 (2016), 599–620, https://doi.org/10.1093/afraf/adw051.

Chauhan, V., 'Lakshmibai and Jhalkaribai: Women Heroes and Contesting Caste and Gender Paradigms and Histories', *South Asian Review* 37:2 (2016), 81–98, https://doi.org/10.1080/02759527.2016.11933063.

Cid, G., '"Amazons in the Pantheon?" Women Warriors, Nationalism and Hero Cults in Nineteenth and Twentieth-Century Chile and Peru', in B. Cothran, J. Judge, and A. Shubert (eds.), *Women Warriors and National Heroes* (London: Bloomsbury, 2020), pp. 199–216.

Cobbs, E., *The Hello Girls: America's First Women Soldiers* (Cambridge, MA: Harvard University Press, 2017).

Cockin, K., 'Cicely Hamilton's Warriors: Dramatic Reinventions of Militancy in the British Women's Suffrage Movement', *Women's History Review* 14: 3–4 (2005), 527–42.

Coleman, M., 'Compensating Irish Female Revolutionaries, 1916–1923', *Women's History Review* 26:6 (2017), 915–34.

Coleman, M., 'Military Service Pensions for Veterans of the Irish Revolution', *War in History* 20:2 (2013), 201–21.

Corbesero, S., 'Femininity (Con)scripted: Female Images in Soviet Wartime Poster Propaganda, 1941–1945', *Aspasia* 4:1 (2010), 103–20.

Cordier, M. and Maggio, R., *Marie Marvingt: La Femme d'un Siècle* (Sarreguemines: Pierron, 1991).

Cothran, B., Judge, J., and Shubert, A. (eds.), *Women Warriors and National Heroes* (London: Bloomsbury, 2020).

Cottam, K. J., 'Soviet Women in Combat in World War II: The Ground Forces and the Navy', *International Journal of Women's Studies* 3:4 (1980), 345–57.

Crang, J. A., *Sisters in Arms: Women in the British Armed Forces during the Second World War* (Cambridge: Cambridge University Press, 2020).

Cross, R. and Miles, R., *Warrior Women: 3000 Years of Courage and Heroism* (London: Quercus, 2011).

Daniels, R. V., *Red October: The Bolshevik Revolution of 1917* (New York: Charles Scribner's Sons, 1967).

Das, S., *India, Empire and First World War Culture* (Cambridge: Cambridge University Press, 2018).

Davies, P., 'Women Warriors, Feminism and National Socialism: The Reception of J.J. Bachofen's view of Amazons among German and Austrian Right-Wing Women Writers', in S. Colvin and H. Watanabe-O'Kelly (eds.), *Women and Death 2: Warlike Women in the German Literary and Cultural Imagination Since 1500* (Rochester, NY: Camden House, 2000), pp. 45–60.

Degroot, G. J. and Peniston-Bird, C. (eds.), *A Soldier and a Woman: Sexual Integration in the Military* (London: Longman, 2000).

Dubois, C., '"A Light in the Path to Us Women of Today": Constance Markievicz's Heroines of the Past', *Imaginaires* 23 (2021), 30–47.

Edwards, L., *Women Warriors and Wartime Spies of China* (Cambridge: Cambridge University Press, 2016).

Eichenberg, J., 'Soldiers to Civilians, Civilians to Soldiers: Poland and Ireland after the First World War', in R. Gerwarth and J. Horne (eds.), *War in Peace: Paramilitary Violence after the Great War* (Oxford: Oxford University Press, 2012), pp. 184–99.

Emen-Gökatalay, G., 'Popularising and Promoting Nene Hatun as an Iconic Turkish Mother in Early Cold War Turkey', *Journal of Middle East Women's Studies* 17:1 (2021), 43–63, https://doi.org/10.1215/15525864-8790224.

Enloe, C., *Does Khaki Become You? The Militarization of Women's Lives* (London: Pluto Press, 1983).

Erll, A., 'Travelling Memory', *Parallax* 17:4 (2011), 4–18.

Fell, A. S., *Women as Veterans in Britain and France after the First World War* (Cambridge: Cambridge University Press, 2018).

Fell, A. S. and Sharp, I. (eds.), *The Women's Movement in Wartime: International Perspectives* (Basingstoke: Palgrave, 2007)

Fidelis, M., *Women, Communism and Industrialisation in Postwar Poland* (Cambridge: Cambridge University Press, 2013).

Filipowicz, H., 'The Daughters of Emilia Plater', in P. Chester, and S. Forrester (eds.), *Engendering Slavic Literatures* (Bloomington, IN: Indiana University Press, 1996), pp. 34–82.

Fitzpatrick Dean, J., *All Dressed Up: Modern Irish Historical Pageantry* (New York: Syracuse University Press, 2014).

Forbes, G., 'Mothers and Sisters: Feminism and Nationalism in the Thought of Subhas Chandra Bose', *Asian Studies* 2: 1 (1984), 23–32.

Gerwarth, R., 'Introduction. Hero Cults and the Politics of the Past: Comparative European Perspectives', *European History Quarterly* 39:3 (2009), 381–87.

Giesbrecht, S., 'Deutsche Liedpostkarten als Propagandamedium im Ersten Weltkrieg', in M. Matter and T. Widmaier (eds.), *Lied und Populare Kultur/ Song and Popular Culture. Jahrbuch des Deutschen Volksliedarchivs*, 50/51 (2006), 55–98.

Grant de Pauw, L., *Battle Cries and Lullabies: Women in War from Prehistory to the Present* (Norman, OK: University of Oklahoma Press, 1998).

Grayzel, S. R., *Women and the First World War* (London: Routledge, 2002).

Grimel, C., 'The American Maid', in D. Goy-Blanquet (ed.), *Joan of Arc: A Saint for All Seasons* (London: Ashgate, 2013), pp. 123–41.

Gucciardo, D. and Howatt, M., 'Sniper Girls and Fearless Heroines: Wartime Representations of Foreign Women in English-Canadian Press, 1941–1943', in B. C. Hacker and M. Vining (eds.), *A Companion to Women's Military History* (Leiden: Brill, 2012), pp. 547–67.

Gullickson, G. L., *Unruly Women of Paris: Images of the Commune* (Ithaca, NY: Cornell University Press, 1996).

Hacker, B. C. and Vining, M. (eds.), *A Companion to Women's Military History* (Leiden: Brill, 2012).

Hagemann, K., Dudink, S. and Rose, S. O. (eds.), *Oxford Handbook of Gender, War and the Western World* (Oxford: Oxford University Press, 2021).

Hagemann, K., Dudink, S. and Tosh, J. (eds.), *Masculinities in Politics and War: Gendering Politics and History* (Manchester: Manchester University Press, 2004).

Hall, R., *Women on the Civil War Battlefront* (Lawrence, KS: University Press of Kansas, 2006).

Hansen, J., 'The Forgotten Front? Serbian Memory and the First World War', in R. B. McCormick, A. Hernandez-Laroche and C. G. Canino (eds.) *An International Rediscovery of World War 1: Distant Fronts* (London: Routledge, 2020), pp. 35–53.

Harris, K., 'Modern Mulans: Reimagining the Mulan Legend in Chinese Film 1920s–1960s', in E. Otto and V. Rocco (eds.), *The New Woman International: Representations in Photography and Film from the 1870s through the 1960s* (Ann Arbor, MI: University of Michigan Press, 2011), pp. 309–30.

Hauser, E., 'Traditions of Patriotism, Question of Gender: The Case of Poland', in E. E. Berry (ed.), *Postcommunism and the Body Politic* (New York: New York University Press, 1995), pp. 78–104.

Heimann, N. M. and Coyle, L., *Joan of Arc: Her Image in France and America* (Washington, DC: Corcoran Gallery of Art, 2006).

Herrmann, G., 'Voices of the Vanquished: Leftist Women and the Spanish Civil War', *Journal of Spanish Cultural Studies* 4:1 (2013), 11–29.

Higonnet, P and Higonnet, M. R., 'The Double Helix', in M. R. Higonnet, J. Jenson, S. Michel and M. Collins Weitz (eds.), *Behind the Lines: Gender and the Two World Wars* (New Haven, CT: Yale University Press, 1987), pp. 31–49.

Hills, C. and Silverman, D. C., 'Nationalism and Feminism in Late Colonial India: The Rani of Jhani Regiment', *Modern Asian Studies* 27:4 (1993), 741–60.

Hockx, M., Judge, J., and Mittler, B., (eds.), *Women and the Periodical Press in China's Long Twentieth Century* (Cambridge: Cambridge University Press, 2018).

Horne, J., (ed.), *State, Society and Mobilisation in Europe in the First World War* (Cambridge: Cambridge University Press, 1997).

Horton, O. R., 'Origin Stories: Rebooting Masculinity in Superhero Films After 9/11', *Human: Journal of Literature & Culture* 6 (2016), 72–85.

Horváth, A. D., 'Of Female Chastity and Male Arms: The Balkan "Man Woman" in the Age of the World Picture', *Journal of the History of Sexuality*, 20:2 (2011), 358–81.

Horváth, A. D., 'An Amazon Warrior, A Chaste Maiden or a Social Man? Early Ethnographic Accounts of the Balkan Man-Woman', *Aspasia* 3:1 (2009), 1–30.

James, P., (ed.), *Picture This: World War 1 Posters and Visual Culture* (Lincoln, NE: University of Nebraska Press, 2009), pp. 273–311.

Jensen, K., *Mobilizing Minerva: American Women in the First World War* (Champaign, IL: University of Illinois Press, 2008).

Krylova, A., *Soviet Women in Combat: A History of Violence on the Eastern Front* (Cambridge: Cambridge University Press, 2010).

Kuzma-Markowska, S., 'Soldiers, Members of Parliament, Social Activists: The Polish Women's Movement after World War 1', in I. Sharp and M. Stibbe (eds.), *Aftermaths of War: Womens' Movements and Female Activists 1918– 1923* (Leiden: Brill, 2011), pp. 265–86.

Larson, L. E., 'Wives and Warriors: The Royal Women of Dahomey as Representatives of the Kingdom', in J. Hobson (ed.), *The Routledge Companion to Black Women's Cultural Histories* (New York: Routledge, 2021), pp. 225–35.

Lebra, J., *Women Against the Raj: The Rani of Jhansi Regiment* (Singapore: Institute of South East Asian Studies, 2008).

Lebra-Chapman, J., *Rani of Jhansi: A Study in Female Heroism in India* (Honolulu, HI: University of Hawaii Press, 1986).

Lepore, J., *The Secret History of Wonder Woman* (New York: Vintage, 2015).

Lintunen, T., 'Women at War', in T. Tepora and A. Roselius (eds.), *The Finnish Civil War 1918* (Leiden: Brill, 2014), pp. 201–29.

Lumsden, L. J., *Inez: The Life and Times of Inez Milholland* (Bloomington, IN: Indiana University Press, 2008).

Maurya, P., and Kumar, N., '*Manikarnika: The Queen of Jhansi* and Its Topicality', *South Asian Popular Culture* 18:3 (2020), 247–60, https://doi .org/10.1080/14746689.2020.1815452.

Mesche, R., *Before Trans: Three Gender Stories from Nineteenth-Century France* (Redwood City, CA: Stanford University Press, 2020).

Moore, B., *Resistance in Western Europe* (Oxford: Berg, 2000).

Nash, M., *Defying Male Civilization: Women in the Spanish Civil War* (Denver, CO: Arden Press, 1995).

Newman, J. P., *Yugoslavia in the Shadow of War: Veterans and the Limit of State Building* (Cambridge: Cambridge University Press, 2015).

Nijhawan, S., *Women and Girls in the Hindu Public Sphere* (Oxford: Oxford University Press, 2011).

Noakes, L., *Women in the British Army: War and the Gentle Sex 1907–1948* (London: Routledge, 2006).

Novikova, I., 'Imagining Africa and Blackness in the Russian Empire: From Extra-textual *arapka* and Distant Cannibals to Dahomey Amazon Shows live in Moscow and Riga', *Social Identities* 19:5 (2013), 571–91, https://doi.org/10.1080/13504630.2013.810122.

Nym Mayhall, L. E., *The Militant Suffrage Movement: Citizenship and Resistance in Britain, 1860–1930* (Oxford: Oxford University Press, 2003).

Paddock, T. (ed.), *World War 1 and Propaganda* (Leiden: Brill, 2014).

Palmer, M. B., *International News Agencies: A History* (Basingstoke: Palgrave Macmillan, 2019).

Pattinson, J., *Women of War: Gender, Modernity and the First Aid Nursing Yeomanry* (Manchester: Manchester University Press, 2020).

Paxton, N., *Stage Rights! The Actresses' Franchise League, Activism and Politics 1908–58* (Manchester: Manchester University Press, 2018).

Pennington, R. (ed.), *From Amazons to Fighter Pilots*, 2 vols. (Westport, CT: Greenwood, 2003).

Perrakis, S., *The Improbable Heroine: Lela Karayanni and the British Secret Services in World War II Greece* (Berlin: De Gruyter, 2022).

Petrone, K., *The Great War in Russian Memory* (Bloomington, IN: Indiana University Press, 2011).

Pike, A. and Cooper, R., *Australian Film 1900–1977: A Guide to Feature Film Production* (Oxford: Oxford University Press, 1998).

Proctor, T., *Female Intelligence: Women and Espionage in the First World War* (New York: New York University Press, 2006).

Qian, N., 'Competing Conceptualisations of Guo (Country, State and/or Nation State) in Late Qing Women's Journals', in M. Hockx, J. Judge and B. Mittler (eds.), *Women and the Periodical Press in China's Long Twentieth Century* (Cambridge: Cambridge University Press, 2018), pp. 217–35.

Ramdani, M., 'Women in the 1919 Egyptian Revolution: From Feminist Awakening to Nationalist Political Activism', *Journal of International Women's Studies* 14:2 (2013), 39–52.

Rath, T., *Myths of Demilitarization in Postrevolutionary Mexico 1920–1960* (Chapel Hill, NC: University of North Carolina Press, 2013).

Regalado, A. J., *Bending Steel: Modernity and the American Superhero* (Jackson, MS: University Press of Mississippi, 2015).

Rettig, T. F., 'Recruiting the All Female Rani of Jhansi Regiment: Subhas Chandra Bose and Dr Lakshmi Swaminadhan', *South East Asia Research* 21: 4 (2013), 627–38.

Rickards, M., *Posters of the First World War* (London: Evelyn, Adams and Mackay, 1968).

Sackeyfio-Lenoch, N., 'Reframing Yaa Asantewaa through the Shifting Paradigms of African Historiography', in J. Hobson (ed.), *The Routledge*

Companion to Black Women's Cultural Histories (New York: Routledge, 2021), pp. 236–44.

Salmonson, J. A., *The Encyclopedia of Amazons: Women Warriors from Antiquity to the Modern Era* (St Paul, MIN: Paragon House Publishers, 1991).

Schubart, R., 'Bulk, Breast and Beauty: Negotiating the Superhero Body in Gal Gadot's Wonder Woman', *Continuum*, 33:2 (2019), 160–72 (p. 164).

Schwartz, P., 'Behind the Lines: Women's Activism in Wartime France', in M. R. Higonnet, J. Jenson, S. Michel and M. Collins Weitz (eds.), *Behind the Lines: Gender and the Two World Wars* (New Haven, CT: Yale University Press, 1987), pp. 141–53.

Sharp, I. and Stibbe, M. (eds.), *Aftermaths of War: Women's Movements and Female Activists 1918–1923* (Leiden: Brill, 2011).

Shlapentok, D., 'The Images of the French Revolution in the February and Bolshevik Revolutions', *Russian History* 16:1 (1989), 31–54.

Shubert, A., 'Women Warriors and National Heroes: Agustina de Aragón and Her Indian Sisters', *Journal of World History* 23:2 (2012), 279–313.

Singh, H., *The Rani of Jhansi: Gender, History and Fable in India* (Cambridge: Cambridge University Press, 2014).

Smith, A. K., *British Women of the Eastern Front: War, Writing and Experience in Serbia and Russia, 1914–20* (Manchester: Manchester University Press, 2016).

Stibbe, M., and Sharp, I., '"In diesen Tagen kamen wir nicht von der Strasse . . ." Frauen in der deutschen Revolution von 1918/19', *Ariadne* 73–74 (2018), 32–29.

Stockdale, M. K., 'My Death for the Motherland is Happiness': Women, Patriotism and Soldiering in Russia's Great War', *The American Historical Review* 109:1 (2004), 78–116.

Stoff, L. S., *They Fought for the Motherland: Russia's Women Soldiers in World War 1 and the Revolution* (Lawrence, KS: University Press of Kansas, 2006).

Summerfield, P. and Peniston-Bird, C., 'Women in the Firing Line: The Home Guard and the Defence of Gender Boundaries in Britain in the Second World War', *Women's History Review* 9:2 (2000), 231–55.

Toler, P. D., *Women Warriors: An Unexpected History* (Boston, MA: Beacon Press, 2019).

Touati, S., 'Lalla Fatma N'Soumner (1830–1863): Spirituality, Resistance and Womanly Leadership in Colonial Algeria', *Societes* 8:4 (2028), 1–16.

Walle, M., 'Fräulein Doktor Elsbeth Schragmüller', *Guerres mondiales et conflits contemporains*, 232 (2008), 47–58.

Walsh, F., *Irish Women and the Great War* (Cambridge: Cambridge University Press, 2020).

Ward, C., '"Something of the Spirit of Stalingrad": British Women, their Soviet Sisters, Propaganda and Politics in the Second World War', *Twentieth Century British History* 25:3 (2014), 435–60.

Warner, M., *Joan of Arc: The Image of Female Heroism* (London: Penguin, 1983).

Warner, M., *Monuments and Maidens: The Allegory of the Female Form* (London: Random House, 2010).

Welch, D. (ed.), *Justifying War: Propaganda, Politics and the Modern Age* (Basingstoke: Palgrave Macmillan, 2012).

Wheelwright, J., *Sisters in Arms: Female Warriors from Antiquity to the New Millenium* (London: Osprey, 2020).

Wingfield, N. and Bucur, M. (eds.), *Gender and War in Twentieth-Century Eastern Europe* (Bloomington, IN: Indiana University Press, 2006).

Wood, E. A., *The Baba and the Comrade: Gender and Politics in Revolutionary Russia* (Bloomington, IN: Indiana University Press, 1997).

Woodward, R. and Duncanson, C. (eds.), *The Palgrave International Handbook of Gender and the Military* (Basingstoke: Palgrave, 2017).

Xiaohong, X., 'Heroines in Late Qing Women's Journals: Meiji-Era Writing on "Women's Self-Help"', in M. Hockx, J. Judge and B. Mittler (eds.), *Women and the Periodical Press in China's Long Twentieth Century* (Cambridge: Cambridge University Press, 2018), pp. 236–54.

Young, A., *Women Who Become Men: Albanian Sworn Virgins* (Oxford: Berg, 2000).

Zhang, Y., *Engendering the Woman Question: Men, Women and Writing in China's Early Periodical Press* (Leiden: Brill, 2020).

Internet Sources

Anon, 'Amelio Robles Ávila', Amelio Robles Ávila | Legacy Project Chicago, https://legacyprojectchicago.org/person/amelio-robles-avila.

Anon, Blog, 'La Serbie s'invite: entretien avec Sladana Zarić', 20 January 2015, http://femmesenuniforme.blogspot.com/2015/01/la-serbie-sinvite-interview-de-slaana.html.

Mladenović, B., 'Women's Mobilization for War (South East Europe)', *1914–1918-online. International Encyclopedia of the First World War*, https://doi.org/10.15463/ie1418.10167.

Clinton, H., email, 22 August 2017, https://still4hill.com/2017/08/22/email-from-hillary-clinton-4/.

Crawford, E., Blog, 'Suffrage Stories: Is this Edith Craig's Banner for the Catholic Women's Suffrage Society?', https://womanandhersphere.com/2019/02/26/suffrage-stories-is-this-edith-craigs-banner-for-the-catholic-womens-suffrage-society/.

Grayzel S. R., and Proctor, T. M., blog, 'Wonder Woman and the Realities of World War 1', https://blog.oup.com/2017/07/wonder-woman-and-world-war-i/.

McElvanney, K., 'Women and the Russian Revolution', www.bl.uk/russian-revolution/articles/women-and-the-russian-revolution.

Museum of London, 'That malignant suffragette: Remembering Emily Davison', www.museumoflondon.org.uk/discover/malignant-suffragette-remembering-emily-wilding-davison.

National Museums of Kenya, 'Mekatilili Wa Menza: The Story of the Giriama Wonder Woman', https://artsandculture.google.com/story/mekatilili-wa-menza-the-story-of-the-giriama-wonder-woman/uQJiyBBzmBOAKg.

Regamey, A., 'Soviet Women Snipers: Experiences of Fire', paper presented at 'Annihilation and Resilience: The Soviet War and PostWar, 1939-1968', Berlin, 29–30 January 2015. www.academia.edu/download/36492911/Soviet_women_snipers_experiences_of_fire.pdf.

Van Den Bosch, W. and Grémaux, R., 'Jeanne Merkus', *Digital Women's Lexicon of the Netherlands*, http://resources.huygens.knaw.nl/vrouwenlexicon/lemmata/data/Merkus.

'Wonder Women & Rebel Girls: Women Warriors in the Media, ca. 1800-present', workshop presented at University College Dublin, 2020, https://wonderwomenworkshop.wordpress.com.

Cambridge Elements ≡

Modern Wars

General Editor
Robert Gerwarth
University College Dublin

Robert Gerwarth is Professor of Modern History at University College Dublin and Director of UCD's Centre for War Studies. He has published widely on the history of political violence in twentieth-century Europe, including an award-winning history of the aftermath of the Great War, *The Vanquished*, and a critically acclaimed biography of Reinhard Heydrich, the chief organizer of the Holocaust. He is also the general editor of Oxford University Press's *Greater War* series, and, with Jay Winter, general editor of Cambridge University Press's *Studies in the Social and Cultural History of Modern* Warfare series.

Editorial Board

About the Series
Focusing on the flourishing field of war studies (broadly defined to include social, cultural and political perspectives), Elements in Modern Wars examine the forms, manifestations, and legacies of violence in global contexts from the mid-nineteenth century to the present day.

Cambridge Elements ☰

Modern Wars

Printed in the United States
by Baker & Taylor Publisher Services